PERANAKAN
SNACKS &
DESSERTS

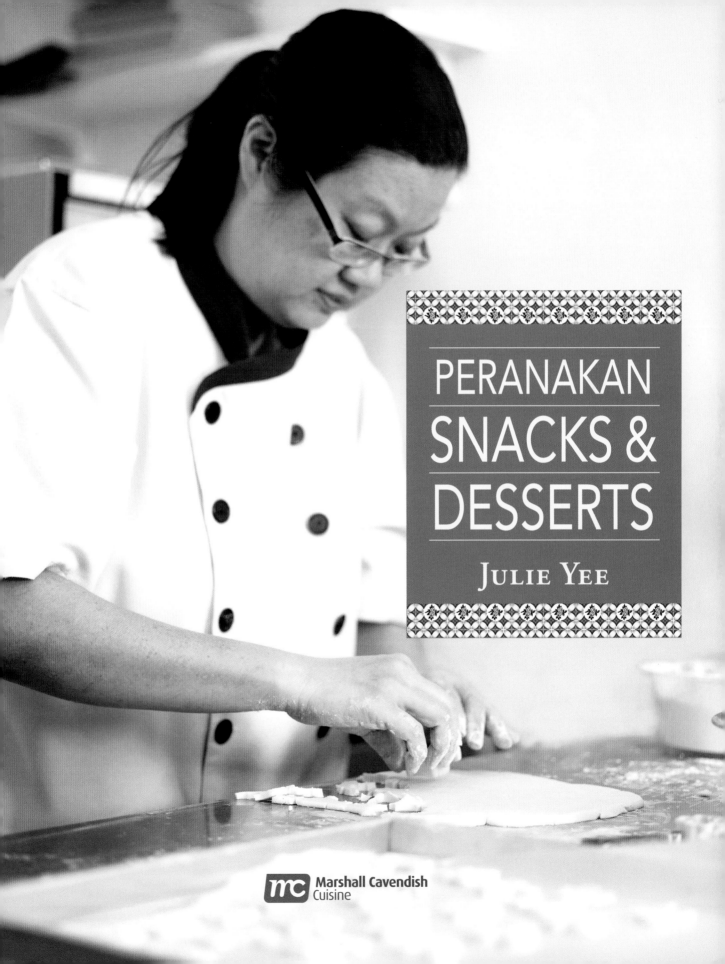

PERANAKAN SNACKS & DESSERTS

JULIE YEE

Marshall Cavendish
Cuisine

Editor: Melissa Tham
Designer: Bernard Go Kwang Meng
Photographer: Calvin Tan

Copyright © 2015 Marshall Cavendish International (Asia) Private Limited
Reprinted 2018

Published by Marshall Cavendish Cuisine
An imprint of Marshall Cavendish International

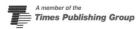
A member of the
Times Publishing Group

Other Marshall Cavendish Offices:
Marshall Cavendish Corporation. 99 White Plains Road, Tarrytown NY 10591-9001, USA ●
Marshall Cavendish International (Thailand) Co Ltd. 253 Asoke, 12th Flr, Sukhumvit 21 Road,
Klongtoey Nua, Wattana, Bangkok 10110, Thailand ● Marshall Cavendish (Malaysia) Sdn Bhd,
Times Subang, Lot 46, Subang Hi-Tech Industrial Park, Batu Tiga, 40000 Shah Alam, Selangor
Darul Ehsan, Malaysia

National Library Board, Singapore Cataloguing-in-Publication Data

Yee, Julie, author.
Peranakan snacks & desserts / Julie Yee. – Singapore : Marshall Cavendish Cuisine, [2014]
pages cm
ISBN : 978-981-45-1622-8 (paperback)
1. Cooking, Peranakan. 2. Snack foods – Malaysia. 3. Desserts – Malaysia. 4. Cookbooks. I. Title.
TX724.5.M4

641.59595 – dc23 OCN879582829

Printed by Times Offset (M) Sdn Bhd

Dedication

I would like to dedicate this book to my grandmother and my mother Patsy,
both of whom have inspired me greatly
and have had immense influences on my culinary style.
I would also like to dedicate this book to
my wonderful family, my husband and lovely children
for their unwavering support.

Contents

Acknowledgements

My grandmother, with her passion and love for cooking for her loved ones, has really inspired me. I really miss those days when my mother, aunties and cousins all chipped in to bake Chinese New Year cookies and helped prepare festival snacks and cookies alongside my grandmother!

My mother, Patsy, for her great eye for detail and her high expectations of baking and cooking, especially her famous *kueh lapis* and chiffon cakes. Her honest appraisals of the food I bake and cook have spurred me on to constantly improve my recipes. I would like to thank her for overseeing my household and kids while I am busy teaching.

My wonderful husband, John, for the support and encouragement that he has given me, especially during tough times. Thank you for being there for me as I continue to pursue my love for baking and cooking.

My three lovely children, Crystal, Nicklaus and Benjamin for their kind understanding. Thank you for being independent when mummy is busy on weekends!

My mentors – Eric Perez of Macaron Pastry Training Center (Bangkok), Judy Koh of Creative Culinaire, Anna Phua of Anna's Culinary Arts and Bong Hiong Hwa of Jia Le Confectionery & Training Centre – for their generous sharing and guidance. They have always been and will always be mentors that inspire me in my teaching career.

My loyal students who have been with me all these years, supporting and encouraging me. Thank you for your understanding and friendship. You guys have injected lots of fun and laughter in my classes. These cherished memories will be forever etched in my heart.

Special thanks to Grace Tan of ToTT for giving me the opportunity to teach at ToTT and also for supporting my teaching and cooking endeavours.

I would also like to thank Teresa and Sherise of Bake King for their ongoing support and for giving me the opportunity to conduct classes at Haig Road.

Not forgetting of course, Marshall Cavendish's excellent team – Lydia, Bernard, Melissa and the marketing team – and photographer Calvin for their understanding, patience and professionalism. They have provided me with a most memorable and rewarding experience and I have learnt so much from them.

Introduction

I felt very happy when I was first approached to do this book, as I thought this would be a most meaningful way of commemorating my grandmother, who shared these treasured recipes with me. You might ask, why Peranakan snacks and desserts? Well, it is simply because I was exposed to them at a very young age! My grandmother would prepare these sweet and savoury treats very often and my aunties also sold *kuehs* for a living. You can even say that I was brought up on *kuehs*!

Growing up, I spent most of my time with my grandmother, watching her cook and helping out whenever she cooked for our large family gatherings. My grandmother would also sell these homemade *kueh* and dumplings during festive seasons. I observed the amount of dedication and love she put into each dish she made. She taught me so much about Peranakan snacks and desserts and I will never forget the wonderful times and memories spent in her cosy little kitchen.

These recipes are simplified to suit the contemporary audience with busy, modern lifestyles. I have sought to simplify traditional methods and recipes with modern equipment such that the cooking process is made much easier but of course, without compromising the traditional authentic Peranakan flavours.

I hope that this beloved collection of mine unravels the mysteries of Peranakan snacks and desserts that have never been shared beyond the Peranakan kitchen and I also hope that many people will be enticed by these recipes and want to learn more about Peranakan *kuehs*.

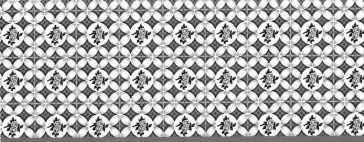

NYONYA KUEH AND SWEET TREATS

Nyonya Kueh Sarlat
Glutinous Rice with Pandan Kaya 12

Pulot Tai Tai with Kaya
Glutinous Rice Cake with Nyonya Kaya 14

Nyonya Ang Ku Kueh
Glutinous Rice Flour Cake with Peanut Filling 16

Kueh Lapis Beras
Nine-layer Kueh 18

Kueh Ambon
Indonesian Honeycomb Cake 20

Pancakes with Durian Sauce 22

Durian Sago Kueh 24

Bingka Ubi Kayu
Baked Tapioca Cake 26

Steamed Pandan Ubi
Steamed Pandan Tapioca Kueh 28

Nyonya Kueh Dadar
Pandan Crêpes with Caramelized Grated Coconut 30

Kueh Ko Swee
Chewy Palm Sugar Cake 32

Gula Melaka Getuk Getuk
Coconut Palm Sugar Tapioca Cake 34

Ondeh Ondeh
Sweet Potato Balls with Palm Sugar Filling 36

Gula Melaka Coconut Candy
Freshly Grated Coconut with Gula Melaka Candy 38

Nyonya Kueh Sarlat

GLUTINOUS RICE WITH PANDAN KAYA

MAKES ONE 20-CM SQUARE CAKE

GLUTINOUS RICE LAYER

300 g glutinous rice, soaked for at least 3 hours and drained

150 ml coconut cream

60 ml +1 Tbsp water

³/₄ tsp salt

5 pandan leaves, rinsed and knotted

cooking oil as needed

BLUE PEA FLOWER WATER

20 blue pea flowers (*bunga telang*), or a few drops of blue food colouring

3 Tbsp water

PANDAN KAYA LAYER

50 ml pandan juice

100 g sugar

1 Tbsp custard powder

50 g rice flour

¹/₄ tsp salt

280 g coconut cream

3 eggs, beaten

1. Prepare glutinous rice layer. In a large bowl, mix soaked and drained glutinous rice with coconut cream, 60 ml water and salt. Spread rice in a steaming tray lined with muslin cloth. Add pandan leaves and steam over high heat for 30 minutes until rice is cooked and tender. Sprinkle 1 Tbsp of water onto rice if the rice is not translucent and steam for another 10 minutes.

2. While rice is steaming, prepare blue pea flower water. Rinse and pound flowers with a mortar and pestle. Add water and mix. Squeeze pounded flowers to extract as much juice as possible.

3. Remove pandan leaves from tray and drizzle blue pea flower water or blue food colouring over rice. Gently mix rice with a fork till blue colouring coats rice evenly.

4. Brush a 20-cm square baking tray with a little oil. Transfer rice to prepared tray and press down with an oiled spatula to flatten and compact rice. Return rice to steamer and leave rice covered in steamer while preparing kaya.

5. Prepare pandan kaya layer. To get pandan juice, rinse and cut 8 pandan leaves into strips of 4-cm. Add 3 Tbsp water and blend till runny. Strain the pandan mixture through a sieve and collect 50 ml pandan juice for use.

6. In a large bowl, mix sugar, custard powder, rice flour, pandan juice, salt and coconut cream until smooth and there are no lumps. Stir in eggs.

7. Pour mixture into a saucepan and cook stirring over medium heat till slightly thickened.

8. Pour thickened mixture over glutinous rice layer. Cover baking tray with a clean dry tea towel and steam at medium-low heat for 25 minutes till kaya sets.

9. Cool *kueh sarlat* thoroughly before cutting into serving slices with oiled knife. *Kueh sarlat* can be stored at room temperature for 1 day.

TIP

- Soaking the glutinous rice helps shorten the cooking time, but do not soak it overnight as the rice will lose its fragrance.

- Steam the kaya over medium-low heat to keep it moist, as high heat will dehydrate the kaya.

- Covering the baking tray with a dry tea towel will prevent water from the condensed steam dripping onto the kaya.

Pulot Tai Tai with Kaya

GLUTINOUS RICE CAKE WITH NYONYA KAYA

MAKES 12 PIECES

BLUE PEA FLOWER WATER

15 blue pea flowers
(*bunga telang*), or
a few drops of
blue food colouring

2 Tbsp water

GLUTINOUS RICE CAKES

300 g glutinous rice,
soaked for 4 hours and drained

190 ml coconut cream

$^1/_4$ tsp salt

$^3/_4$ Tbsp castor sugar

oil as needed

NYONYA KAYA

50 ml pandan juice

220 g sugar

280 ml coconut cream

10 egg yolks

1. Prepare blue pea flower water. Rinse and pound flowers with a mortar and pestle. Add water and mix. Squeeze pounded flowers to extract as much juice as possible. Set aside.

2. Prepare glutinous rice cakes. In a large bowl, mix soaked and drained glutinous rice with coconut cream, salt and castor sugar. Spread rice in a steaming tray lined with muslin cloth and steam for 30 minutes until rice is cooked and tender.

3. Spoon one-third of steamed rice into a bowl and sprinkle with blue pea flower water or blue food colouring. Mix well and return rice to tray to steam for another 5 minutes.

4. Brush tart moulds with a little oil. Remove rice from steamer and press into moulds, starting with half the uncoloured rice, then the blue-coloured rice and topping with the remaining uncoloured rice. Press down with an oiled spatula to flatten and compact rice. Set aside to cool. Leave rice to cool for an hour before slicing with oiled knife. *Pulot tai tai* can be kept refrigerated for 2 days.

5. Prepare nyonya kaya. To get pandan juice, rinse and cut 8 pandan leaves into strips of 4-cm. Add 3 Tbsp water and blend till runny. Strain the pandan mixture through a sieve and collect 50 ml pandan juice for use.

6. Mix sugar with coconut cream and pandan juice in a heatproof bowl. Boil in a double boiler until sugar has dissolved.

7. Beat egg yolks in a mixing bowl. Gradually add half the warm coconut cream mixture while stirring. Return mixture to the heatproof bowl and stir constantly over simmering water for 15 minutes to prevent lumps from forming and until mixture is smooth and firm.

8. Leave kaya to cool completely before storing in clean, dry airtight jars. Keep refrigerated. Kaya can be kept refrigerated for 3 weeks.

9. Serve with glutinous rice cakes.

TIP

- To ensure that the glutinous rice cooks evenly, stir it after 15 minutes of steaming.

- For traditional looking *pulot tai tai*, press rice on a greased, banana leaf-lined tray instead.

Nyonya Ang Ku Kueh

GLUTINOUS RICE FLOUR CAKE WITH PEANUT FILLING

MAKES 10 PIECES

banana leaves as needed, lightly oiled and cut into small squares

PEANUT FILLING
200 g peanuts, chopped

90 g sugar

1 Tbsp white sesame seeds

2 Tbsp hot water

SWEET POTATO DOUGH
80 g sweet potatoes

30 g rice flour

100 ml water

50 ml + 1 Tbsp corn oil

20 ml pandan juice

180 g glutinous rice flour + more for dusting

60 ml coconut milk

60 ml milk

1. Prepare peanut filling. In a bowl, mix peanuts with sugar, sesame seeds and hot water. Mix well and shape into small balls, each about 25 g. Place in a covered container and set aside.

2. Prepare sweet potato dough. Steam sweet potatoes until tender. Peel and mash coarsely. Set aside.

3. Mix rice flour, water and 1 Tbsp corn oil in a small non-stick pan. Cook, stirring over low heat, until mixture thickens. Remove from heat and set aside.

4. To get pandan juice, rinse and cut 8 pandan leaves into strips of 4-cm. Add 3 Tbsp water and blend till runny. Strain the pandan mixture through a sieve and collect 20 ml pandan juice for use.

5. Using an electric mixer, combine glutinous rice flour with sweet potato mash, 50 ml corn oil and pandan juice. Add rice flour mixture and mix well. Add coconut milk and milk, then knead to get a smooth and pliable dough.

6. With oiled hands, divide dough into small balls, each about 12 g. Flatten a ball of dough and top with 25 g peanut filling. Bring the edges of the dough up to enclose the filling and pinch to seal. Roll between your palms to form a smooth ball. Repeat with the rest of the balls of dough.

7. Dust *ang ku kueh* mould with some glutinous rice flour and press a ball of dough firmly into the mould. Turn the mould over and knock it gently to release the dough. Place dough on a small square of banana leaf and arrange on a steaming tray. Repeat with the rest of the balls of dough.

8. Steam *ang ku kueh* for 7 minutes. Lift steamer lid halfway through steaming to release some heat, then replace lid.

9. Remove *ang ku kueh* from heat. Cool slightly before serving. *Kueh* can be kept refrigerated for 2 days.

TIP

- Lifting the steamer lid halfway through steaming (after about $3^1/_2$ minutes) will help prevent the *ang ku kueh* from over-expanding.

- Besides peanut filling, you can also fill the *ang ku kueh* with red bean paste or mung bean paste.

Kueh Lapis Beras

NINE-LAYER KUEH

MAKES ONE 20-CM SQUARE CAKE

oil as needed

75 g rice flour

375 g tapioca flour

1 tsp salt

1.12 litres coconut milk

320 g sugar

6 pandan leaves, rinsed and knotted

$^1/_4$ tsp each of green and red food colouring

1. Brush a 20-cm square baking tray with a little oil. Set aside.

2. In a large bowl, mix rice flour, tapioca flour and salt with 800 ml coconut milk. Stir till mixture is smooth and there are no lumps. Set aside.

3. Place the remaining 320 ml coconut milk, sugar and pandan leaves in a saucepan and stir over low heat till sugar is dissolved. Remove pandan leaves and stir sweetened coconut milk into rice flour mixture. Mix well.

4. Divide batter into three equal portions. Leave one portion uncoloured and add green and red food colouring to the other two portions. Mix each portion well. Set aside a small amount of red coloured batter for the final layer.

5. Ladle batter randomly into prepared tray to form a thin, even layer. Steam for 5 minutes till batter is set. Ladle a different coloured batter over the first layer and steam for 5 minutes till second layer sets. Repeat with the next batter. Alternate the colours randomly and steam the layers, making sure that each layer is set before adding the next. Ladle the reserved red coloured batter as the final layer.

6. Steam for 20 minutes. Allow *kueh* to cool for an hour before cutting into serving slices with oiled knife.

7. *Kueh* can be kept refrigerated for 1 month. Bring *kueh* to room temperature before serving.

TIP

- Do not over boil the coconut milk, as the heat will separate the coconut oil from the milk.

- To ensure that the layers adhere, the subsequent layer must be added while the previous layer is still warm.

- To ensure that the layers are even and the colours do not run, each layer must be set before a new layer is added.

Kueh Ambon

INDONESIAN HONEYCOMB CAKE

MAKES ONE 22-CM SQUARE CAKE

180 ml fresh or canned coconut water

35 g all-purpose flour

35 g rice flour

235 g sugar

9 g instant yeast

360 ml coconut cream

$1/4$ tsp salt

50 g egg whites

180 g egg yolks

40 g butter, melted

270 g tapioca flour or sago flour, sifted

1. Preheat bottom heating element in oven to 170°C for 20 minutes. Line a 22-cm square baking tray with baking paper. Set aside.

2. In a large bowl, mix coconut water, all-purpose flour, rice flour, 15 g sugar and instant yeast into a thick batter. Set aside to prove for 30 minutes.

3. In a saucepan, warm coconut cream over low heat. Add 120 g sugar and salt and stir until sugar is dissolved. Set aside to cool to 40°C.

4. In a mixing bowl, whisk egg whites, egg yolks and remaining 100 g sugar by hand for 8 minutes till sugar is dissolved and mixture is slightly fluffy.

5. Add coconut cream mixture and melted butter to mixing bowl, then mix well. Add sifted tapioca or sago flour and mix again. Stir in yeast mixture.

6. Cover batter with a damp tea towel and set aside to prove for 3 hours or till batter is dotted with air bubbles.

7. Pour batter into prepared tray and bake at 170°C (bottom heat) for 1 hour, opening oven door every 15 minutes to release excess heat.

8. Turn on top heating element to 180°C and increase bottom heating element to 180°C. Bake for another 12 minutes till top of cake is golden brown.

9. Remove from oven and leave to cool on a wire rack before cutting into serving slices with oiled knife. The cake can be kept refrigerated for 3 days.

Pancakes with Durian Sauce

MAKES 10 PANCAKES

PANCAKES
220 ml milk

4 egg yolks

1 tsp baking powder

120 g cake flour

$^1/_4$ tsp salt

1 tsp vanilla powder

4 egg whites

30 g sugar

cooking oil as needed

DURIAN SAUCE
80 g fresh durian purée

20 g palm sugar
(*gula melaka*), chopped

50 ml coconut milk

50 ml milk

120 ml water

1 tsp cornflour

1. Prepare pancakes. Whisk milk and egg yolks together in a large bowl. Add baking powder, cake flour, salt and vanilla powder and mix well. Set aside.

2. In a clean mixing bowl, whisk egg whites and sugar to soft peaks.

3. Combine egg yolk and egg white mixtures and leave to rest for 10 minutes.

4. Heat a little oil in a non-stick frying pan over medium heat. Ladle 1 small scoop of batter onto pan. Cook until batter is set, then flip it over to cook the other side. Transfer pancake to a plate and cover with a damp cloth. Repeat to make more pancakes until batter is used up.

5. Prepare durian sauce. In a small saucepan over low heat, combine durian purée and palm sugar with coconut milk, milk, water and cornflour. Stir until sugar is dissolved and mixture is smooth. Allow mixture to come to the boil over low heat, then remove from heat and set aside to cool.

6. Serve pancakes with durian sauce. Durian sauce and pancakes can be kept for one day at room temperature.

Durian Sago Kueh

MAKES ONE 23-CM SQUARE CAKE

oil as needed

65 ml coconut milk

65 ml milk

100 g sugar

150 g sago pearls, soaked for 30 minutes and drained

20 g wheat starch

250 g durian flesh

STEAMED GRATED COCONUT

200 g grated skinned coconut

1/2 tsp salt

1. Brush a 23-cm round baking tray with a little oil. Set aside.

2. Prepare steamed grated coconut. Line a steaming tray with muslin cloth. Sprinkle grated coconut with salt and place in the steaming tray to steam for 5 minutes. Set aside to cool.

3. Place coconut milk, milk and sugar in a small saucepan and bring to a boil, stirring until sugar is dissolved. Pour into a large heatproof bowl. Add soaked and drained sago and mix well, followed by wheat starch and durian flesh. Mix well.

4. Pour mixture into prepared tray and steam for 40 minutes.

5. Cut *kueh* into long strips immediately using an oiled kitchen scraper while hot and serve with steamed grated coconut. *Kueh* can be kept refrigerated for 2 days.

TIP
- Soaking the sago allows the sago pearls to double in size and also prevents them from clumping together. Do not stir the sago while soaking as the stirring action could dissolve the sago pearls.

Bingka Ubi Kayu

BAKED TAPIOCA CAKE

MAKES ONE 18-CM SQUARE CAKE

oil as needed

350 ml coconut cream

160 g sugar

1/4 tsp salt

4 pandan leaves, rinsed and knotted

50 g butter

1 tsp vanilla extract

650 g grated tapioca

50 g grated skinned coconut

30 g tapioca flour

10 g wheat starch

1 egg, beaten

1 egg yolk, beaten with a pinch of salt

1. Brush an 18-cm square baking tray with a little oil, then line with banana leaf or baking paper and oil lightly.

2. In a saucepan over low heat, place coconut cream, sugar, salt and pandan leaves and stir until sugar is dissolved. Add butter and vanilla extract and mix well. Remove pandan leaves and set mixture aside.

3. In a large bowl, mix together grated tapioca, grated coconut, tapioca flour, wheat starch and egg. Add coconut cream mixture and mix well. Return mixture to the saucepan and cook over low heat until mixture is sticky.

4. Pour mixture into prepared tray, level it and steam for 30 minutes over high heat.

5. Preheat oven to 190°C. Brush top of steamed cake with beaten egg yolk and bake for 45 minutes until cake is evenly brown.

6. Cool cake for 15 minutes and cut into serving slices with an oiled kitchen scraper. Cake can be kept for 2 days refrigerated.

TIP

• To make pandan-flavoured tapioca cake, add 50 ml pandan juice and reduce the amount of coconut cream by 50 ml in step 2.

• I would advise buying ready-grated tapioca from the market to simplify the process. Grated tapioca can be stored in the freezer for up to 3 months.

Steamed Pandan Ubi
STEAMED PANDAN TAPIOCA KUEH

MAKES ONE 20-CM SQUARE CAKE

banana leaves as needed,
to cover 20-cm square tray

500 g grated tapioca

200 ml water

70 ml pandan juice

100 ml coconut milk

150 g sugar

STEAMED GRATED COCONUT

200 g grated skinned coconut

1/2 tsp salt

1. Prepare steamed grated coconut. Line a steaming tray with muslin cloth. Sprinkle grated coconut with salt and place in the steaming tray to steam for 5 minutes. Set aside to cool.

2. Place tapioca in a large heatproof bowl and set aside. Line a 20-cm square baking tray with banana leaves or a thick sheet of plastic and oil lightly. Set aside.

3. To get pandan juice, rinse and cut 8 pandan leaves into strips of 4-cm. Add 3 Tbsp water and blend till runny. Strain the pandan mixture through a sieve and collect 70 ml pandan juice for use.

4. In a saucepan, bring water, pandan juice, coconut milk and sugar to the boil, stirring until sugar is dissolved.

5. Add hot pandan syrup to tapioca and stir until mixture is starchy.

6. Pour mixture into prepared tray and steam for 30–45 minutes until mixture is set. Leave *kueh* to cool in tray for 15 minutes before cutting.

7. Cut *kueh* into cubes with oiled kitchen scraper. Coat with steamed grated coconut before serving. *Kueh* can be kept refrigerated for 2 days.

TIP

- To make a multi-layered tapioca cake, divide the mixture into 3 portions and add a different food colouring to each portion. Steam the first layer for 10 minutes, then add the next layer and steam for another 10 minutes. Repeat for the third layer and steam until the cake is set.

- To check if the cake is thoroughly cooked, insert a toothpick into the centre of cake. It should come out clean.

Nyonya Kueh Dadar

PANDAN CRÊPES WITH CARAMELIZED GRATED COCONUT

MAKES 6 PIECES

CRÊPES

2 Tbsp pandan juice

140 g all-purpose flour

2 Tbsp tapioca flour

200 ml coconut cream

200 ml water

2 eggs, beaten

1¹/₂ tsp salt

1 tsp pandan paste

cooking oil as needed

FILLING

120 g palm sugar
(*gula melaka*), chopped

2 Tbsp water

240 g grated skinned coconut

¹/₂ tsp salt

2 Tbsp tapioca flour

1. Prepare filling. In a saucepan over low heat, cook palm sugar with water until sugar is dissolved, stirring to prevent burning. Add grated coconut, salt and tapioca flour and stir-fry lightly till coconut is caramelized and moist.

2. To get pandan juice, rinse and cut 8 pandan leaves into strips of 4-cm. Add 3 Tbsp water and blend till runny. Strain the pandan mixture through a sieve and collect 2 Tbsp pandan juice for use.

3. Prepare crêpes. In a large bowl, whisk together all-purpose flour, tapioca flour, coconut cream, water, eggs, salt, pandan juice and pandan paste to obtain a smooth batter. Pour batter through a sieve to remove any lumps and set aside to rest for at least 30 minutes.

4. Heat a little oil in a 24-cm non-stick frying pan over medium heat. Add 1 Tbsp batter and swirl the pan quickly so batter coats the base of pan. Cook until batter is set, then flip it over to cook the other side. Remove crêpe to a plate. Cover with a damp towel. Repeat to make more crêpes until batter is used up.

5. To make *kueh dadar*, spread 2 Tbsp coconut filling in the middle of a crêpe. Fold lower edge of crêpe over the filling, then fold left and right sides over and roll up. Repeat until crêpes and filling are used up.

6. Serve *kueh dadar* warm. *Kueh* can be kept at room temperature for 1 day.

TIP

- This may require a bit of practice, but the crêpes should be thin so that the texture would not be too doughy.

- Stir-frying the filling helps to bring out the fragrance of the coconut, but be careful not to overcook the mixture or it would be too dry.

- For neat and presentable rolls, keep the crêpes uniform and roll them as tightly as possible.

Kueh Ko Swee

CHEWY PALM SUGAR CAKE

MAKES ONE 15-CM SQUARE CAKE

100 g palm sugar (*gula melaka*), chopped

20 g sugar

a pinch of salt

420 ml water

6 pandan leaves, rinsed and knotted

50 g tapioca flour

50 g rice flour

$^1/_3$ tsp alkaline water or finely pounded orange lye

STEAMED GRATED COCONUT

250 g grated skinned coconut

$^1/_4$ tsp salt

2 pandan leaves, rinsed and knotted

1. Prepare steamed grated coconut. Line a steaming tray with muslin cloth. Sprinkle grated coconut with $^1/_4$ tsp salt and place into steaming tray. Top with pandan leaves and steam for 10 minutes. Set aside to cool.

2. Combine palm sugar, sugar, salt, 240 ml water and pandan leaves in a saucepan and boil for 5 minutes until sugar is dissolved. Set aside. Remove pandan leaves.

3. In a bowl, mix tapioca flour, rice flour and alkaline water or pounded orange lye with 180 ml water. Whisk to form a smooth batter. Pour batter into saucepan with sugar syrup and mix well.

4. Set mixture over low heat and whisk until thick and viscous. Remove from heat and continue whisking until mixture is cool and batter falls off the whisk smoothly and in a ribbon-like pattern.

5. Line a 15-cm square baking tray with lightly oiled baking paper, then smooth the lined tray with a wet spatula.

6. Transfer batter into prepared tray and steam for 10 minutes over high heat until batter is set. Remove from heat and set aside to cool.

7. Cut *kueh* into squares with an oiled kitchen scraper after 10 minutes.

8. Coat *kueh* with steam grated coconut and serve. *Kueh ko swee* can be kept for one day at room temperature.

TIP
- In Singapore and Malaysia, orange lye is available from market stalls that sell dried sundry goods. Sized like a ping-pong ball, orange lye is irregularly shaped and has a hard texture. Pound finely before use. Orange lye gives this *kueh* its elastic texture.

- It may be tiring to whisk the batter, but whisking adds to the *kueh's* springy and elastic texture.

Gula Melaka Getuk Getuk

COCONUT PALM SUGAR TAPIOCA CAKE

MAKES ONE 20-CM SQUARE CAKE

500 g tapioca, washed and peeled

100 g palm sugar (*gula melaka*), chopped

cooking oil as needed

STEAMED GRATED COCONUT

100 g grated skinned coconut

$^1/_4$ tsp salt

1. Prepare steamed grated coconut. Line a steaming tray with muslin cloth. Sprinkle grated coconut with salt and place in the steaming tray to steam for 5 minutes. Set aside to cool.

2. Bring tapioca to a boil for 25 minutes until tender. Drain.

3. Place boiled tapioca in a bowl and mash coarsely, so there are still chunks of tapioca bits visible. Remove and discard the stringy vein. Add palm sugar and mix until sugar is completely dissolved.

4. Mix in all the ingredients together by hand.

5. Brush a 20-cm baking tray with some oil. Spoon the tapioca mash into the prepared tray, then press down using the back of a spoon to compress it. Chill cake in refrigerator for an hour until it sets and is compact.

6. Cut cake into pieces with oiled knife and coat with steamed grated coconut before serving. Cake can be kept refrigerated for 2 days.

TIP
- It is easier to mash the tapioca while it is still hot as the texture is still soft.
- Steaming grated coconut with salt allows the cake to last longer.

Ondeh Ondeh

SWEET POTATO BALLS WITH PALM SUGAR FILLING

MAKES 12 PIECES

200 g sweet potatoes

110 g glutinous rice flour

60 ml hot water

1 Tbsp sugar

a pinch of salt

120 g palm sugar
(*gula melaka*),
finely chopped

6 pandan leaves,
rinsed and knotted

STEAMED GRATED COCONUT

100 g grated skinned coconut

$^1/_4$ tsp salt

1. Prepare steamed grated coconut. Line a steaming tray with muslin cloth. Sprinkle grated coconut with salt and place in the steaming tray to steam for 5 minutes. Set aside to cool.

2. Steam sweet potatoes until tender. Peel and mash.

3. Place sweet potato mash, glutinous rice flour, hot water, sugar and salt into mixer and whisk until a smooth dough is obtained.

4. Apportion dough into 12 small balls, each about 10 g. Set aside in a covered container for 10 minutes.

5. Flatten a ball of dough with your hands and top with 10 g palm sugar. Bring the edges of the dough up to enclose the sugar and pinch to seal. Roll between your palms to form a smooth ball. Repeat until the ingredients are used up.

6. Bring a pot of water to the boil. Add pandan leaves and simmer over medium heat for 10 minutes. Remove pandan leaves and set aside to cool.

7. Add sweet potato balls and cook over medium heat until they float to the surface. Do this in batches to avoid overcrowding the pot.

8. Remove the balls with a slotted spoon and drain well. Coat with steamed grated coconut while the balls are still hot. Serve immediately. *Ondeh ondeh* can be kept for 1 day at room temperature.

TIP
- It is very important to seal the balls well and ensure that they do not have any crack lines, or the palm sugar will seep out during boiling.

- Once the balls float to the surface, remove them. Do not overcook the balls or boil them over too high heat as they will split open.

Gula Melaka Coconut Candy

FRESHLY GRATED COCONUT WITH GULA MELAKA CANDY

MAKES ONE 18-CM SQUARE CAKE

oil as needed

400 g skinned grated coconut

150 g condensed milk

100 g palm sugar (*gula melaka*)

¼ tsp salt

50 g butter

½ tsp vanilla paste

1. Brush a little oil on an 18-cm square tray. Set aside.

2. Combine grated coconut, condensed milk, palm sugar and salt in a pot and cook over low heat for 30 minutes until mixture becomes thick.

3. Add butter and vanilla paste and continue to stir until mixture is pasty and does not stick to the sides of the pot.

4. Transfer mixture to prepared tray. Lightly press the top of the mixture to level it.

5. Chill in refrigerator for 30 minutes or until candy has set and is compact before cutting into 2-cm squares.

6. Store in clean, dry airtight jars. The candy can be stored for 3 months.

TIP
- A possible variation is to replace *gula melaka* with sugar. Divide the mixture into a few portions and add food colouring to each portion for multiple colours.

CAKES, TARTS AND COOKIES

Classic Butter Cake

MAKES ONE 20-CM BUNDT

380 g butter
220 g castor sugar
340 g eggs, beaten
1 tsp vanilla essence or powder
2 tsp lemon juice
130 ml evaporated milk
220 g self-raising flour, sifted

1. Preheat oven to 160°C for 20 minutes. Line a 20-cm bundt pan with baking paper. Set aside.

2. In a mixing bowl, cream butter and castor sugar until mixture is light and fluffy. Add beaten eggs, vanilla essence or powder and lemon juice gradually and mix well.

3. Add one-third of the evaporated milk and sifted flour and fold gently until the mixture is smooth and well-combined. Repeat two more times with the remaining evaporated milk and flour.

4. Pour batter into prepared bundt pan and bake for 40 minutes (fan mode on) until cake is evenly brown.

5. Using oven gloves or a dry tea towel, remove cake from oven and leave to cool slightly on wire rack before unmoulding. Cake can be kept at room temperature for 5 days. If refrigerated, cake can be kept for a week. To serve, remove cake from refrigerator and set aside to cool to room temperature.

TIP
- Using quality pure butter will best bring out the fragrance of the butter cake.

- Adding in the eggs too quickly will cause the mixture to curdle. The addition of 2 Tbsp of flour will help to eliminate the curdling, ensuring that the mixture is smooth and free of clumps.

Egg White Mocha Marbled Cake

250 g butter

180 g sugar

2 tsp vanilla essence or powder

330 g cake flour

250 g evaporated milk

8 egg whites

80 g castor sugar

2 tsp coffee paste

1. Preheat oven to 170°C for 20 minutes. Line a 20-cm square cake tin with lightly oiled baking paper. Set aside.

2. In a large bowl, cream butter and castor sugar until mixture is light and fluffy. Add vanilla essence or powder and mix well. Divide flour and evaporated milk into 4 portions and add them into the bowl, alternating each time.

3. In a clean mixing bowl, whisk egg whites and castor sugar to soft peaks. Add one-third of egg whites to batter and mix lightly. Repeat with remaining egg whites.

4. Spoon one-third of batter into another bowl. Add coffee paste and mix well.

5. Spoon a big ladle of plain mixture into the middle of the cake tin followed by another big ladle of coffee mixture. Repeat alternating mixtures until ingredients are used up.

6. Bake at 170°C for 45 minutes (fan mode on) until golden brown.

7. Using oven gloves or a dry tea towel, remove cake and place on wire rack to cool slightly before unmoulding. Cake can be kept at room temperature for 3 days. If refrigerated, cake can be kept for 5 days. To serve, remove cake from refrigerator and set aside to cool to room temperature.

TIP

- The coffee paste can be substituted with instant coffee granules diluted with $^1/_2$ Tbsp hot water.

- Besides coffee paste, you can also use chocolate paste if you prefer a richer chocolate taste for your cake.

Walnut Cake with Chocolate Rice

MAKES ONE 20-CM ROUND CAKE

200 g butter
180 g sugar
3 eggs
1 egg yolk
$^1/_4$ tsp salt
1 tsp vanilla paste
160 g cake flour
1$^1/_2$ tsp baking powder
$^1/_2$ tsp cinnamon powder
8 Tbsp evaporated milk
60 g walnuts, chopped
30 g chocolate rice

1. Preheat oven to 180°C for 20 minutes. Line a 20-cm round cake tin with lightly oiled baking paper. Set aside.

2. Using an electric mixer, cream butter and sugar for 5 minutes until mixture is cool and creamed mixture falls off the whisk smoothly and in a ribbon-like pattern. Add eggs, egg yolk, salt and vanilla paste separately and mix gently.

3. Sift cake flour, baking powder and cinnamon powder together. Add to butter mixture and mix lightly. Add evaporated milk, walnuts and chocolate rice, then gently fold mixture in with a spatula.

4. Pour batter into prepared tin and bake at 180°C for 30 minutes or until cake is golden brown and centre is thoroughly cooked.

5. Using oven gloves or a dry tea towel, remove cake from oven and leave to cool on a wire rack. Set aside.

6. Cake can be kept at room temperature for 3 days. If refrigerated, cake can be kept for a week. To serve, remove cake from refrigerator and set aside to cool to room temperature.

TIP
- A dropping consistency is essential for the creamed mixture as it ensures that the cake is moist. Test with a spoon. Dip the spoon into the mixture and gently shake the mixture off. You would have achieved the desired dropping consistency if the mixture falls off the spoon easily. Adding one more spoonful of evaporated milk can help to soften the mixture.

- The butter and egg yolk have to be at the same temperature before they can be combined in order for the buttercream mixture to be smoothly emulsified.

Fresh Pandan Chiffon Cake

MAKES ONE 23-CM CAKE

110 g egg yolks
250 g sugar
60 ml corn oil
30 ml pandan juice
80 ml coconut cream, hot
$^1/_2$ tsp salt
1 tsp pandan paste
190 g cake flour, sifted
300 g egg whites
1 tsp lemon juice

1. Preheat oven at 170°C for 20 minutes. Prepare a 23-cm chiffon cake tin. Set aside.

2. Prepare yolk mixture. In a mixing bowl, whisk egg yolks, 110 g sugar and corn oil by hand until mixture is smooth. Set aside.

3. To get pandan juice, rinse and cut 8 pandan leaves into strips of 4-cm. Add 3 Tbsp water and blend till runny. Strain the pandan mixture through a sieve and collect 30 ml pandan juice for use.

4. Combine coconut cream, salt, pandan paste and pandan juice and mix well. Add sifted cake flour and mix again.

5. Prepare egg white mixture. Whisk egg whites lightly with mixer. Add lemon juice and 140 g sugar, then gently whisk to stiff peaks.

6. Fold in egg yolk mixture and mix well.

7. Pour batter into prepared cake tin and bake at 170°C on the lower shelf for 40 minutes.

8. Using oven gloves or a dry tea towel, remove and turn cake tin upside down and leave to cool on a wire rack for 1 hour. When cool enough to handle, run a thin bladed knife or a palette knife around the sides of the pan and centre core to release the cake. Run knife along the base of the pan to remove cake.

9. Cut into desired number of slices and serve. Cake can be kept refrigerated for 1 day. To serve, remove cake from refrigerator and set aside to cool to room temperature.

TIP
- You can replace lemon juice with cornflour.
- Do not over fold the mixture, as the meringue will lose its airy texture with the constant stirring.

Orange Chiffon Cake

MAKES ONE 23-CM CAKE

5 egg yolks

170 g castor sugar

1 tsp orange oil or paste

100 ml ready-packed orange juice
or juice extracted from 2 oranges

1 Tbsp lemon juice

$1/2$ tsp orange zest, finely grated

110 g cake flour, sifted

$1/2$ tsp salt

190 g egg whites

2 tsp cornflour

1. Preheat oven to 170°C for 20 minutes. Prepare a 23-cm chiffon cake tin. Set aside.

2. In a small bowl, whisk egg yolks, 70 g castor sugar and orange oil or paste together by hand until mixture is thick.

3. Add orange juice, lemon juice and orange zest together and mix well, then add sifted cake flour and salt and mix.

4. In a separate bowl, whisk egg whites, remaining 100 g castor sugar and cornflour to stiff peaks.

5. Fold egg yolk mixture into egg white mixture with spatula, then mix until batter is well-combined.

6. Pour batter into prepared chiffon cake tin and bake at the lower shelf for 170°C (fan on) for 60 minutes until cake is slightly golden brown.

7. Using oven gloves or a dry tea towel, remove and turn cake tin upside down and leave to cool on a wire rack for 1 hour. When cool enough to handle, run a thin bladed knife or a palette knife around the sides of the pan and centre core to release the cake. Run knife along the base of the pan to remove cake.

8. Cut into desired number of slices and serve. Cake can be kept refrigerated for 3 days. To serve, remove cake from refrigerator and set aside to cool to room temperature.

Classic Kueh Lapis

LAYERED CAKE

MAKES ONE 18-CM SQUARE CAKE

380 g butter, cold
160 g icing sugar
3 egg whites
27 egg yolks
3 Tbsp brandy
4 Tbsp condensed milk
30 g all-purpose flour + more for dusting
2-3 tsp *lapis* spices or cake spices

1. Preheat oven at 250°C for 20 minutes. Line an 18-cm square cake tin with baking paper and dust some flour on it.

2. In a large bowl, cream cold butter and 80 g icing sugar until mixture is light and fluffy and butter is not yet melted. Set aside.

3. In an electric mixer, beat egg whites with remaining icing sugar to stiff peaks. Add egg yolks one by one into mixer and cream until mixture is light and creamy. Add brandy and condensed milk and mix well.

4. Turn mixer to lowest speed and add creamed butter mixture.

5. Sift all-purpose flour and *lapis* spices or cake spices together in a separate bowl. Add flour mixture into mixer and fold by hand.

6. To build cake layers, spread 3 spoonfuls of mixture evenly in the prepared cake tin.

7. Bake at 250°C for 3–5 minutes until cake layer is golden brown. Prick cake gently with toothpick to check for bubbles and remove any excess air. Press baked layer flat with a parchment paper.

8. Spread another 2–3 spoonfuls of mixture and bake again. Repeat process until batter is used up.

9. Bake with top and bottom heating element at 200°C for 5 minutes if cake sides are slightly sticky. Brush cake with brandy generously while still warm.

10. Remove cake from oven and leave to cool on a wire rack. Slice into pieces and serve. Cake can be kept refrigerated for 1 month.

TIP

• To make *kueh lapis* fruitcake, put brandy-soaked prunes and caramelized banana on every 2 or 3 layers.

• Avoid opening the oven door unnecessarily to check on the new layers as this will lead to a longer baking time and a drier cake.

Almond Sugee Cake

SEMOLINA CAKE

MAKES ONE 23-CM SQUARE CAKE

200 g semolina flour
340 g butter
170 ml condensed milk
3 egg whites
120 g sugar
8 egg yolks
40 g all-purpose flour
80 g almonds, grounded
1 Tbsp brandy (optional)
almond flakes as needed, for decoration

1. Preheat oven at 160°C for 20 minutes. Line a 23-cm square cake tin with lightly oiled baking paper. Set aside.

2. Whisk semolina flour, butter and condensed milk in a large bowl until white and creamy. Allow mixture to rest for 20 minutes.

3. In a separate bowl, whisk egg whites and sugar to soft peaks. Add egg yolks and whisk until fluffy.

4. Combine egg mixture and semolina flour mixture together and mix well.

5. Fold all-purpose flour, almonds and brandy (if used) into the flour and egg mixture and mix well.

6. Pour cake mixture into the prepared cake tin and bake at 160°C for 45 minutes (fan mode on) until golden brown.

7. Remove cake from oven and leave to cool on a wire rack. Cut into desired number of slices and serve with almond flakes on top. Cake can be kept refrigerated for 1 week. To serve, reheat cake at 160°C for 10 minutes.

TIP

- It is important that the semolina flour mixture has sufficient resting time in order for the flour to retain its moisture and to be fully softened.

- The brandy can easily be substituted with orange juice.

- The cake tastes best 3 days after baking as the oil in the semolina flour would have been released and would elevate the fragrance and taste of the cake.

Silky Custard Egg Tarts

MAKES 6 TARTS

TART BASE
90 g butter

50 g sugar

1 egg

180 g all-purpose flour

SUGAR SYRUP
60 g sugar

170 ml water

2 slices lemon

SILKY CUSTARD FILLING
3 eggs

1 egg yolk

$1/_4$ tsp vinegar

100 ml milk

1. Prepare tart base. In a large bowl, cream butter and sugar together for 5 minutes until mixture is well blended and fluffy. Stir in egg. Add all-purpose flour to the mixture gently and gradually, using a spatula to fold flour in with horizontal sweeping motions until dough is obtained.

2. Divide dough into small round balls and press into 6-cm tart moulds.

3. Place tart moulds on a 20-cm tray and arrange them such that the moulds are spaced apart. Bake in oven for 8 minutes at 180°C until tart shells are golden brown. Remove from oven and set aside to cool while preparing sugar syrup.

4. Prepare sugar syrup. Combine sugar with water and lemon slices and boil for 5 minutes. Set aside to cool.

5. Prepare silky custard filling. In a large bowl, beat eggs, egg yolk and vinegar together. Add sugar syrup and milk and pour mixture through a strainer.

6. Fill tart shells with custard filling until three-quarters full. Cover with a cake tray on top.

7. Bake at 170°C for 10 minutes, until custard sets and is soft in the centre. Remove from oven and leave to cool on a wire rack for 15 minutes before serving. Egg tarts can be kept refrigerated for 3 days. To serve, reheat tarts at 160°C for 8 minutes.

TIP

- Do not overbeat dough or the tart will turn out too crumbly.

- Baking custard at a high temperature leads to the egg-milk emulsion separating and turning into curds.

Gula Melaka Coconut Tarts

MAKES 6 TARTS

green and red
maraschino cherries
as needed, for decoration

TART BASE
90 g butter

50 g sugar

1 egg

160 g all-purpose flour

COCONUT FILLING
250 g grated skinned coconut

100 ml *gula melaka* syrup

1 egg

40 g melted butter or olive oil

20 g milk powder

1 tsp water

1 egg yolk, beaten

1. Prepare tart base. In a large bowl, cream butter and sugar together for 5 minutes until mixture is well blended and fluffy. Stir in egg. Add all-purpose flour to the mixture gently and gradually, using a spatula to fold flour in with horizontal sweeping motions until dough is obtained.

2. Divide dough into small round balls and press into 6-cm tart moulds.

3. Place tart moulds on a 20-cm tray and arrange them such that the moulds are spaced apart. Bake in oven for 8 minutes at 180°C until tart shells are golden brown. Set aside while preparing coconut filling.

4. Prepare coconut filling. Combine grated coconut, *gula melaka* syrup, egg, melted butter or olive oil, milk powder and water in a large bowl and mix well.

5. Put a tablespoonful of coconut filling evenly into the tart shells. Repeat until coconut filling is used up.

6. Brush top of coconut tart with beaten egg yolk and bake at 180°C for about 20 minutes or until coconut filling is golden brown.

7. Remove from oven and leave to cool on a wire rack for 10 minutes before serving. Decorate with maraschino cherries on top. Coconut tarts can be kept refrigerated for 3 days. To serve, reheat at 160°C for 8 minutes.

TIP
- *Gula melaka* syrup is available at supermarkets such as NTUC Fairprice.

- The brand of the milk powder does not need to be specific.

Almond Sugee Cookies

SEMOLINA COOKIES

MAKES 180 PIECES

400 g all-purpose flour

1^1/$_2$ tsp double action baking powder

1^1/$_2$ tsp baking soda

130 g icing sugar

^{1}/$_2$ tsp salt

100 g almonds, ground

^{1}/$_4$ tsp ammonia powder

2 tsp water

270 g butter or ghee (optional), melted

2 egg yolks

1. Preheat oven to 170°C for 20 minutes. Line a baking tray with baking paper. Set aside.

2. In a large bowl, combine all-purpose flour, baking powder, baking soda with icing sugar and salt. Mix well. Add ground almonds and mix well.

3. Mix ammonia powder with 1 tsp water and add to mixture. Add melted butter or ghee (if used). Mix well and fold until the mixture achieves a dough consistency. Let dough rest for 1 hour.

4. Pinch and divide dough into small round balls and arrange them on the prepared baking tray spaced 3-cm apart.

5. Prepare egg glaze. Mix egg yolk with 1 tsp water and glaze sugee balls. Bake at 170°C for 20 minutes or until cookies are light brown.

6. Remove from oven and leave to cool completely on wire rack before serving. Store cookies in clean, dry airtight jars. Sugee cookies can be kept for 1 month.

TIP

• As the cookies will expand to more than three times their size while baking, the dough balls need to be spaced 3-cm apart.

• Ammonia powder in the recipe gives cookies a a soft and delicate texture that melts easily in the mouth.

• The cookies taste best 3 days after baking as the oil in the semolina flour would have been released and would elevate the fragrance and taste of the cookies.

Kueh Bangkit

TAPIOCA AND SAGO FLOUR COCONUT COOKIES

MAKES 240 COOKIES

300 g tapioca flour +
more for dusting

400 g sago flour

8 pandan leaves,
rinsed dry and knotted

240 ml coconut cream

a pinch of salt

240 g sugar

3 egg yolks

1. Preheat oven to 165°C for 20 minutes. Line a tray with lightly oiled baking paper and dust some flour on it. Set aside.

2. In a wok, fry tapioca flour and sago flour with pandan leaves over medium heat for 20 minutes until flour is light and fragrant. Stir continuously to prevent flour from burning at the bottom of wok. Remove flour from wok and set aside to cool. Sift cooled flour and set aside.

3. In a bowl, combine coconut cream with salt and 120 g sugar and mix well.

4. In another bowl, whisk egg yolks with remaining 120 g sugar for 5 minutes until thick and gradually stir in coconut cream mixture. Whisk well until sugar is dissolved. Pour in sifted flours and knead to get a soft and pliable dough. Cover dough with a damp tea towel.

5. Take a handful of dough and roll out to 0.5-cm thickness on a floured surface. Use cookie moulds to cut out desired patterns, then pinch the top of each cookie with pastry pincers. Add a small portion of new dough to the leftover dough which would be drier, before rolling out. Place cookies on prepared tray. Leave cookies to dry for 15 minutes before baking.

6. Bake at 160°C for about 20 minutes or until cookies are completely dry. The base should be light brown and the top white.

7. Remove from oven and leave to cool on wire rack before serving. Store cookies in clean, dry airtight jars. *Kueh bangkit* can be kept for 1 month.

TIP
- If the dough gets too dry while mixing, add coconut milk. This not only provides moisture but also gives the dough more flavour.

- *Kueh bangkit* cookies taste best 2 or 3 days after baking as the coconut oil in the cookies would have been released and to enhance the taste of the cookies.

- If sago flour is not available, substitute with tapioca flour.

- Allowing the cookies to rest before baking ensures that the patterns on the cookies are more visible. You can also bake the flour in the oven at 150°C for 30 minutes.

Daisy Butter Cookies

MAKES 80 COOKIES

125 g butter
100 g icing sugar
1 egg
1 tsp vanilla paste
150 g all-purpose flour
25 g milk powder
$^1/_4$ tsp baking soda
green and red maraschino cherries as needed, for decoration

1. Preheat oven at 170°C for 20 minutes. Line baking tray with baking paper. Set aside.

2. In an electric mixer, whisk butter and icing sugar at low speed until creamy. Add egg and vanilla paste and mix well.

3. In a bowl, sift all-purpose flour, milk powder and baking soda.

4. Fold sifted flour mixture into butter mixture with a spatula.

5. Transfer combined mixture into a piping bag fitted with a rosette nozzle and pipe the cream onto the prepared tray. With one hand holding the piping bag, use the other to squeeze out sufficient cream. Form jagged petals by rotating the bag clockwise and anti-clockwise.

6. Cut maraschino cherries into small pieces and place a small piece in the middle of each flower dough.

7. Bake for 15 minutes (top and bottom heat with fan on) or until cookies are golden brown.

8. Remove and leave on wire rack to cool. Store cookies in an airtight jar. The cookies can be kept for 1 month.

TIP

• Use quality pure butter to best bring out the fragrance of the cookies.

• Do not overmix the flour or the cookies will be dry and tough.

• The cookies taste best after 3 days as the oil in the butter would have been released and would add to the fragrance and taste of the cookies.

Nyonya Pineapple Tarts

MAKES 75 TARTS

TART BASE
220 g all-purpose flour
1 Tbsp milk powder
140 g butter
40 g sugar
1 egg
1 egg yolk
1 tsp vanilla extract

PINEAPPLE FILLING
4 pineapples
2 cinnamon sticks
4 pandan leaves, rinsed and knotted
2 slices lemon
250 g yellow rock sugar
1 Tbsp maltose (optional)

1. Preheat oven at 170°C for 20 minutes. Line tray with baking paper. Set aside.

2. Prepare tart base. Sift all-purpose flour and milk powder together and set aside.

3. In a large bowl, cream butter and sugar together for 5 minutes until mixture is well blended and fluffy. Add egg, egg yolk and vanilla extract and beat for another 5 minutes. Add sifted flour and milk powder and mix well until a soft pliable dough is obtained.

4. Chill dough in the refrigerator for 20 minutes.

5. Take a handful of dough and roll out to 0.5-cm thickness. Lay dough on prepared tray. Use a pineapple tart mould to cut out the tart bases. Repeat until dough is used up. Pinch the edges of the tarts with pastry pincers. Following that, press out tiny star patterns with star mould. Repeat until there are sufficient stars for the tart bases. Set aside while preparing pineapple filling.

6. Prepare pineapple filling. Skin pineapples and remove eyes. Using a grater, grate pineapple until the core is left. Put pineapple in a sieve and let the juice drain for 15 minutes.

7. In a saucepan, cook pineapple pulp, cinnamon sticks, pandan leaves and lemon slices over low heat. Add rock sugar and simmer until almost dry. Add maltose, if used, and cook for another 10 minutes. Stir continuously to prevent flour from burning at the bottom of the pan. Remove pandan leaves.

8. Remove pineapple jam from heat and transfer to a small bowl to cool. Make a slight depression at the centre of the tart base and fill with pineapple jam. Place star cut-outs on top of pineapple jam.

9. Bake at 170°C for 20 minutes (fan mode on) or until base is light brown.

10. Using oven gloves or a dry tea towel, remove from oven and leave to cool on wire rack before serving. Pineapple tarts can be stored in airtight containers for 1 month.

TIP
- Do not overwork the pastry dough as this will toughen the dough when the gluten is formed.

- The sweetness of the pineapple filling can be adjusted by the amount of sugar added. It is best to taste the pineapple filling first before adding more sugar.

Nyonya Crispy Kueh Bolu
CRISPY MOULDED SPONGE CAKES

MAKES 100 SMALL PIECES

5 eggs

280 g sugar

$^1/_2$ tsp vanilla powder

all-purpose flour as needed

6 pandan leaves, rinsed and knotted

melted butter or coconut oil as needed

1. Preheat oven to 200°C for 20 minutes.

2. In a mixing bowl, whisk eggs, sugar and vanilla powder until fluffy. Weigh the amount of batter to calculate the amount of all-purpose flour needed in the next step. It should be 70 g flour for every 200 g batter.

3. In a small pan, fry all-purpose flour with pandan leaves until flour is lightly roasted and fragrant. Remove pandan leaves from pan.

4. Transfer flour to a separate bowl. Ensure that flour and batter have been weighed accurately. Fold in flour with batter, alternating until batter is well mixed.

5. Heat *kueh bolu* mould till very hot in the oven. Use oven gloves and remove mould from oven. Grease generously with melted butter or coconut oil.

6. Fill prepared mould with batter until three-quarters full. Place in oven to bake at 200°C for 10 minutes or until golden brown.

7. Remove mould from oven and leave to cool on wire rack before turning out cakes. *Kueh bolu* can be kept in airtight containers for 2 weeks at room temperature.

TIP

- It is important that you weigh the flour and mix it with the right proportion of batter to ensure that the *kueh bolu* rises well.

- The amount of sugar is what gives *kueh bolu* its signature crispy outer layer so reducing it will result in *kueh bolu* that is not crispy.

- Keeping the *kueh bolu* for 2 days will give it a more crispy texture.

SAVOURY SNACKS

Nyonya Sweet Rice Dumpling

MAKES 30 DUMPLINGS

BLUE PEA FLOWER WATER

20 blue pea flowers
(*bunga telang*)

3 Tbsp water

GLUTINOUS RICE

1 kg glutinous rice

$^1/_2$ Tbsp five-spice powder

1 Tbsp coriander powder

$^1/_2$ Tbsp salt

1 Tbsp ground white pepper

$^1/_2$ Tbsp sugar

2 Tbsp shallot oil

2 Tbsp garlic, peeled and chopped

PORK MARINADE

750 g shoulder butt or pork belly,
cut into cubes

1 Tbsp five-spice powder

6 Tbsp coriander powder

1 tsp salt

1 Tbsp ground white pepper

2 Tbsp dark soy sauce

2 Tbsp light soy sauce

2 Tbsp sugar

DUMPLING FILLING

1 Tbsp shallot oil

50 g garlic, peeled and chopped

70 g dried shrimps

80 g mushrooms

200 g winter melon

$^1/_2$ cup mushroom water

5 Tbsp shallot crisps

80 g chestnuts

WRAPPING

bamboo leaves as needed

pandan leaves as needed, cut into
small rectangular pieces

bamboo strings as needed

1. Prepare blue pea flower water. Rinse and pound flowers with a mortar and pestle. Add water and mix. Squeeze pounded flowers to extract as much juice as possible.

2. Prepare glutinous rice. Soak rice in a basin of water for 4 hours. Drain well. Sprinkle blue pea flower water onto 200 g glutinous rice. Add glutinous rice ingredients to uncoloured glutinous rice. Set aside.

3. Marinate pork belly in pork marinade ingredients. Set aside.

4. Prepare dumpling filling. Heat shallot oil in a wok and sauté garlic until fragrant. Add dried shrimps and mushrooms and fry until fragrant. Add marinated pork and fry for 5 minutes until cooked. Add winter melon and mushroom water, fry, then remove from heat.

5. Transfer filling to a plate. Sprinkle shallot crisps.

6. Prepare wrapping. Overlap two bamboo leaves together and fold into a cone. *(Step 2 on page 74)*

7. Place $1^1/_2$ Tbsp glutinous rice and $^1/_2$ Tbsp coloured rice into the cone. Press down to pack tightly, forming a little depression in the middle. Fill hollow with 2 Tbsp of filling and chestnut, then top with another $1^1/_2$ Tbsp glutinous rice and $^1/_2$ Tbsp coloured rice. Add a small piece of pandan leaf before folding bamboo leaf down to wrap around the dumpling. *(Steps 3–10 on page 74)*

8. Tie with a bamboo string and knot it tightly around the middle of each dumpling. Repeat until ingredients are used up. *(Steps 11–12 on page 74)*

9. Boil dumplings in a pot of hot water for about 1.5 hours or pressure cook for about 30–40 minutes.

10. Remove dumplings from heat and hang up to dry. Dumplings can be kept in the freezer for a month.

TIP
- Soaking the glutinous rice helps shorten the cooking time, but do not soak it overnight as the rice would lose its fragrance.

- It is very important to tie the dumplings tightly so that the boiling water will not seep into the filling.

Hokkien Savoury Fried Rice Dumpling

MAKES 30 DUMPLINGS

GLUTINOUS RICE
1 kg glutinous rice

1 Tbsp five-spice powder

3 Tbsp coriander powder

1 Tbsp salt

1 Tbsp ground white pepper

2 Tbsp sugar

1 Tbsp dark soy sauce

2 Tbsp light soy sauce

pandan leaves as needed

3 Tbsp shallot oil

60 g shallots

60 g garlic

PORK MARINADE
750 g chunky shoulder butt or pork belly, cut into cubes

2 Tbsp five-spice powder

3 Tbsp coriander powder

1 tsp salt

2 tsp ground white pepper

2 Tbsp dark soy sauce

2 Tbsp light soy sauce

1 Tbsp Hua Tiao wine

DUMPLING FILLING
1 Tbsp shallot oil

80 g shallots

60 g garlic

60 g dried shrimps

60 g mushrooms

100 g winter melon

$1/2$ cup mushroom water

2 Tbsp shallot crisps

15 salted egg yolks, cut into halves

WRAPPING
bamboo leaves as needed

1. Prepare glutinous rice. Soak rice in a basin of water for 4 hours. Drain well. Add remaining ingredients and set aside for 30 minutes.

2. Fry pandan leaves in pan till fragrant.

3. Heat shallot oil in a wok and sauté shallots and garlic until light golden brown and fragrant. Add glutinous rice and fry for 5 minutes. Remove from heat and transfer rice to a clean plate. Set aside.

4. Marinate shoulder butt or pork belly in pork marinade ingredients. Set aside.

5. Prepare dumpling filling. Heat shallot oil in the same wok and fry shallots and garlic until golden brown and fragrant. Add dried shrimps and mushrooms. Add marinated pork and winter melon and fry for 5 minutes. Add mushroom water and simmer for 10 minutes until pork is completely cooked.

Continues on page 76

Continues from page 75

6. Remove from heat and transfer filling to a plate. Sprinkle shallot crisps.

7. Prepare wrapping. Overlap two bamboo leaves together and fold into a cone. (*Refer to step-by-step photos on page 74*)

8. Place a tablespoonful of glutinous rice into the cone. Press down to pack tightly, forming a little depression in the middle. Fill hollow with $1^1/_2$ tablespoonful of filling and salted egg yolk, then top with another tablespoonful of glutinous rice. Fold leaf down to wrap around the dumpling.

9. Tie with a bamboo string and knot it tightly around the middle of each dumpling. Repeat until ingredients are used up.

10. Boil dumplings in a pot of hot water for about 1.5 hours or pressure cook for about 30 minutes.

11. Remove dumplings from heat and hang up to dry. Dumplings can be kept in the freezer for a month.

TIP
- Soak bamboo leaves overnight to soften leaves for easy wrapping.
- You can also add 100 g chestnuts and 2 pieces of Chinese sausages to the filling ingredients.

Kee Chang

LYE WATER DUMPLING

MAKES 25 DUMPLINGS

1 tsp orange lye or alkaline water

water as needed

600 g glutinous rice

2 Tbsp cooking oil

500 g red bean paste (optional)

1. Pound orange lye in a mortar and pestle till powdery. Add a little water and mix well.

2. Wash glutinous rice in several changes of water until water runs clear. Stir in orange lye or alkaline water mixture and leave aside to soak for 4 hours.

3. Drain glutinous rice well and add oil. Mix well.

4. Prepare wrapping. Overlap two bamboo leaves together and fold into a cone.

5. Place a tablespoonful of glutinous rice into the cone. Press down to pack tightly, forming a little depression in the middle. Fill the hollow with red bean paste, if using, and top with another tablespoonful of glutinous rice. Fold leaf down to wrap around the dumpling.

6. Tie with a bamboo string and knot tightly around the middle of each dumpling. Repeat until ingredients are used up.

7. Boil the dumplings in a pot of hot water for about 2–2.5 hours or pressure cook for about 40 minutes.

8. Serve with sugar.

TIP

- It is important to select only the pure glutinous rice grains to ensure that the dumpling has a nice yellow colour.

- Lotus paste or kaya can be added as a filling to provide variation to the recipe.

Char Siew Shao Bao

MAKES 15 PIECES

white sesame seeds
as needed, to garnish

SWEET DOUGH

60 g butter

180 g cake flour

50 g icing sugar

70 ml water

PLAIN DOUGH

60 g butter

180 g all-purpose flour

70 ml water

EGG WASH

1 egg

2 Tbsp water

a pinch of salt

1. Preheat oven to 180°C for 20 minutes. Line a 28 x 36-cm cookie tray with parchment paper. Set aside.

2. Prepare sweet dough. In a small bowl, cut butter into cubes and drop into cake flour. Using your fingers, gently rub butter cubes into the flour, breaking them into smaller pieces. *(Steps 2–3 on page 82)*

3. Add icing sugar and water gradually and mix until the batter forms a soft dough. Leave dough to chill in refrigerator for 60 minutes. *(Steps 4–6 on page 82)*

4. Prepare plain dough. In a separate bowl, cut butter into cubes and drop into all-purpose flour. Using your fingers, gently rub butter cubes into the flour, breaking them into smaller pieces. *(Steps 2–3 on page 82)*

5. Add water gradually and mix together until the batter forms a soft dough. Cover with cling-wrap and leave dough to chill in refrigerator for 60 minutes. *(Steps 4-6 on page 82)*

6. Roll chilled dough into sheets of a rectangular size. Plain dough should measure 45 x 15-cm and sweet dough should measure 30 x 15-cm. Place sweet dough on top of plain dough. *(Step 7 on page 82)*

7. Fold one-third of plain dough upwards to cover half of sweet dough, then proceed to fold both into thirds. Turn dough 90° anti-clockwise after folding. Roll dough out again into a long rectangular sheet. Repeat folding into thirds until dough is well-blended. *(Steps 8-10 on page 82)*

8. Roll dough out to 0.3-cm thickness on a floured surface. *(Step 11 on page 82)*

9. Use an 8-cm pastry mould to cut out dough. Tuck in a ball of filling with left thumb, then gently plait the edge using right thumb and index finger, ensuring that it is well sealed. *(Step 12 on page 82)*

10. Place buns on prepared trays. Brush the top of the buns with egg wash, then sprinkle with white sesame seeds.

11. Bake at 180°C for about 20 minutes or until buns are golden brown. Leave to cool on a wire rack before serving. The *char siew shao baos* can be kept refrigerated for 3 days. Reheat before serving.

Char Siew

CHAR SIEW

30 g sugar

$^1/_2$ Tbsp light soy sauce

$^3/_4$ Tbsp oyster sauce

$^1/_2$ Tbsp hoisin sauce

$^1/_2$ tsp Chinese wine

$^1/_2$ tsp ground white pepper

$^1/_4$ tsp five-spice powder

1 Tbsp sesame oil

250 g shoulder butt pork

FILLING

250 g *char siew*, chopped

1 tsp shallots, peeled and chopped

1 tsp garlic, peeled and chopped

1 tsp parsley, chopped

1 Tbsp oyster sauce

$^1/_4$ tsp ground white pepper

1 tsp cornstarch

40 ml *char siew* sauce or water

1. Prepare *char siew*. In a large bowl, combine sugar, light soy sauce, oyster sauce, hoisin sauce, Chinese wine, ground white pepper, five-spice powder and sesame oil and mix until sugar dissolves. Add pork and marinate for at least 4 hours or overnight. Set aside.

2. Prepare filling. In a pan, cook *char siew* and marinade over medium heat for 15 minutes or until cooked. Remove from heat and set aside on a clean plate.

3. In the same pan, fry shallots and garlic until fragrant. Add *char siew*, parsley, oyster sauce and ground white pepper and continue to fry.

4. Mix cornstarch with *char siew* sauce or water and pour into pan.

5. Stir until it comes to a boil and remove from fire. Transfer filling to a medium bowl.

6. Divide filling into 15 portions and shape into balls. Set aside to cool completely until needed.

TIP

- Marinated *char siew* can be refrigerated for future use as a filling or to complement rice as a main dish.

- Oyster sauce can also be replaced with hoisin sauce if preferred.

Nyonya Curry Puff

MAKES 16 PIECES

CHICKEN FILLING

1 onion, peeled and sliced

2 Tbsp curry paste

100 g chicken thigh, cut into cubes

250 g potatoes, peeled, boiled and cut into cubes

2 Tbsp mixed vegetables

1 tsp light soy sauce

1 tsp sugar

cooking oil, as needed

OIL DOUGH

100 g cake flour

70 g butter

WATER DOUGH

100 g shortening

250 g all-purpose flour

20 g sugar

45 ml water

1. Prepare chicken filling. Heat oil in a wok over medium heat and sauté onion until light brown and fragrant.

2. Add curry paste and continue to fry. Add chicken cubes, potatoes, mixed vegetables, light soy sauce and sugar and fry until chicken is cooked.

3. Remove from heat. Leave chicken filling aside to cool until needed.

4. Prepare oil dough. In a bowl, combine cake flour and butter together and mix well. Knead with hands until a soft dough forms. Chill for 30 minutes. (*Refer to step-by-step photos on page 83*)

5. Prepare water dough. Gently break shortening into cubes and drop into flour. Using your fingers, rub the shortening into the flour, breaking them into smaller pieces. Add sugar and water gradually until the batter forms a soft dough. Cover with cling-wrap and leave to chill in refrigerator for 30 minutes.

6. Roll chilled dough into sheets of a rectangular size. Plain dough should measure 45 x 15-cm and oil dough should measure 30 x 15-cm. Place oil dough on top of plain dough.

7. Fold one-third of plain dough upwards to cover half of oil dough, then proceed to fold both into thirds. Turn dough 90° anti-clockwise after folding. Roll dough out again into a long rectangular sheet. Repeat folding into thirds until dough is well-blended.

8. Roll dough out to 0.5-cm thickness on a floured surface and cut into rounds with 10-cm round pastry cutter.

9. Put an equal amount of chicken filling on each round of pastry. Fold into half and seal the sides by pinching and twisting the edges.

10. Heat oil in a wok over medium heat. Gently lower curry puffs into oil and deep-fry until pastry is thoroughly cooked or until golden brown.

11. Remove from heat and transfer to a plate lined with absorbent paper towels. Serve immediately.

TIP

- It is important to deep-fry the curry puffs over medium heat as high heat will make the puffs burst.

- Curry puff fillings can be prepared a day ahead and chilled until needed.

Nyonya Pork Satay

MAKES 48 STICKS

700 g pork

100 g pork lard

bamboo sticks as needed

REMPAH

12 shallots

6 cloves garlic

6 candlenuts

2 stalks lemongrass, sliced

4 slices galangal

3 Tbsp coriander powder

2 tsp fennel powder

1 tsp cumin powder

1 tsp turmeric powder

$^1/_4$ tsp cinnamon powder

6 Tbsp sugar

1 tsp salt

$^1/_2$ Tbsp dark soy sauce

2 Tbsp light soy sauce

1 Tbsp oil

1. Preheat oven to 240°C for 20 minutes. Line oven tray with aluminium foil.

2. Cut pork and pork lard into cubes.

3. Combine *rempah* ingredients in a mortar and pestle and pound till fine.

4. Mix pork cubes and *rempah* and leave to marinate for at least 4 hours.

5. Thread sufficient marinated meat and one cube of lard to cover three-quarters of oiled bamboo stick.

6. Grill satay on top shelf at 240°C (no-fan mode), turning over each side after 5 minutes so that the meat grills evenly.

7. Serve hot with peanut sauce. *(Refer to recipe on page 90)*

TIP
• Chicken can be used as well.

Nyonya Beef and Mutton Satay

MAKES 48 STICKS

600 g beef or mutton
2 Tbsp tamarind
120 ml water
bamboo sticks as needed

REMPAH
16 shallots
6 cloves garlic
6 candlenuts
2 stalks lemongrass, sliced
4 slices ginger
4 slices galangal
3 Tbsp coriander powder
1 tsp cumin powder
1 tsp turmeric powder
6 Tbsp sugar
1^1/$_2$ tsp salt
2 Tbsp oil

1. Preheat oven to 240°C for 20 minutes. Line oven tray with aluminium foil.

2. Cut beef or mutton into cubes.

3. Combine *rempah* ingredients in a mortar and pestle and pound till fine.

4. Mix beef or mutton cubes and *rempah* and leave to marinate for at least 4 hours.

5. Mix tamarind and water together then add to marinated meat.

6. Thread sufficient amount of meat onto oiled bamboo stick.

7. Grill satay on top shelf at 240°C (no-fan mode), turning over each side after 5 minutes so that the meat grills evenly.

8. Serve hot with peanut sauce. *(Refer to recipe on page 90)*

Nyonya Satay Peanut Sauce

3 stalks lemongrass

120 g tamarind

1.06 litres water

500 g peanuts,
coarsely grounded

100 g palm sugar
(*gula melaka*)

4 Tbsp sugar

1 tsp salt

REMPAH

30 dried chillies

160 g shallots

80 g garlic

6 candlenuts

12 slices galangal

4 tsp coriander powder

1 Tbsp *belacan*

200 ml oil

1. In a food processor, blend *rempah* ingredients together.

2. Heat oil in a wok over high heat until it smokes. Stir-fry *rempah* and lemongrass until fragrant.

3. Add tamarind and 160 ml water and continue to stir-fry.

4. Add peanuts, remaining 900 ml water, palm sugar, sugar and salt into wok and fry. Simmer until sauce thickens.

5. Serve hot with satay.

Nyonya Satay Pineapple Sauce

1 pineapple

3 tsp sugar

2 tsp kalamansi lime juice

$^1/_2$ tsp salt

2 red chillies, finely sliced

1. Skin pineapples and remove eyes.

2. Grate pineapple and drain excess juice.

3. Mix grated pineapple, sugar, lime juice and salt together in a small bowl. Garnish with chilli slices.

4. Serve with satay.

Nyonya Otah

MAKES 20 PIECES

3 eggs

250 g coconut cream

50-100 ml water

1 Tbsp cornflour

2 tsp sugar

1 tsp salt

$^1/_2$ Tbsp finely chopped kaffir lime leaf

$^1/_2$ Tbsp finely chopped turmeric leaf,

500 g mackerel (yellow tail fish)

banana leaves as needed, cut into 20 sheets of 16 cm x 22-cm

REMPAH

150 g shallots

80 g garlic

60 g turmeric

20 g *belacan*

30 g ginger

1 stalk lemongrass, sliced (use 6 cm from the bottom)

3 Tbsp chilli paste

1 tsp coriander powder

1 tsp cumin powder

1. Blend *rempah* ingredients in a food processor until smooth.

2. Add eggs, coconut cream, water, cornflour, sugar, salt, kaffir lime leaf and turmeric leaf and blend into a paste.

3. Take 350 g mackerel meat and slap it against the inside of a bowl for 5 minutes until the paste becomes springy. If the texture is too dry, add a bit of water to get a softer texture. Add remaining mackerel and mix well.

4. Place 2-3 Tbsp of fish mixture onto a banana leaf and fold 2 opposite sides inwards and tuck the other 2 sides underneath to get a rectangular pack. Wrap neatly and fasten with a toothpick. Repeat until ingredients are used up.

5. Steam for 10 minutes or grill in oven at 200°C for 10 minutes.

6. Serve immediately.

TIP

- Throwing the fish paste against the side of a bowl creates a more springy elastic texture in the otah.

- The amount of water to be added to the fish paste depends on the softness preferred. Pan-fry a spoonful of fish paste to test the texture of the *otah*.

Paper-wrapped Pandan Chicken

MAKES 12 PIECES

3 chicken thigh fillets

12 parchment bags

pandan leaves as needed,
cut into 5-cm pieces

6 Chinese mushrooms,
soaked and cut into halves

2 chillies, sliced thinly

SEASONING

2 Tbsp garlic,
peeled and minced

1 Tbsp ginger juice

2 Tbsp oyster sauce

2 Tbsp cooking wine

1 Tbsp light soy sauce

1 tsp dark soy sauce

1 tsp sugar

1 tsp sesame oil

1 tsp cornflour

1 tsp ground white pepper

1. Preheat oven to 200°C for 20 minutes. Line tray with baking paper.

2. Wash and remove visible fat from the chicken and cut each fillet into 8 pieces.

3. In a large bowl, combine seasoning ingredients and mix well. Add chicken and toss well, then marinate for at least 4 hours or overnight.

4. Lay one parchment bag on a clean surface. Place one pandan leaf, two pieces of chicken, Chinese mushroom and one chilli in the middle, making sure to keep the filling in the centre.

5. Fold each parchment bag before securing the loose end with a toothpick.

6. Bake packages at 200°C for 15 minutes or until the chicken is completely cooked.

7. Remove from oven and transfer to a plate lined with absorbent paper towels.

8. Serve warm.

TIP
- You can purchase parchment bags from shops selling plastic bags in the wet market.

- For a healthier option, steam the chicken packages instead.

Fried Spring Rolls

MAKES 20 PIECES

20 *popiah* skins

cornstarch water as needed

TURNIP FILLING

cooking oil as needed

2 pieces beancurd, cut into strips

1 Tbsp garlic, peeled and minced

1 Tbsp shallots, peeled and minced

1 Tbsp dried shrimps

1 medium-sized turnip or yam bean, peeled and finely julienned

1 carrot, shredded

1/4 flower cabbage, shredded

50 g chives, cut into strips of 2-cm

200 g minced pork (optional)

SEASONING

1 Tbsp light soy sauce

1 Tbsp oyster sauce

1 Tbsp cooking wine

1 tsp fish sauce

1/2 tsp ground white pepper

1/4 tsp five-spice powder

1/2 tsp sugar

1. Heat 1 cup oil in a non-stick frying pan and sear beancurd until golden. Remove from heat and set aside on a clean plate.

2. Prepare turnip filling. Heat 3 Tbsp of oil in the same pan and add garlic, shallots and dried shrimps. Fry until fragrant.

3. Add turnip or yam bean, carrot, cabbage, chives and beancurd and fry for 10 minutes.

4. Add minced pork, if using, and stir for 3 minutes to prevent sticking or burning at the bottom.

5. Add seasoning and simmer turnip filling till soft and liquid is absorbed.

6. Drain till dry before removing from pan. Transfer filling to a plate and set aside to cool slightly before use.

7. Place 2 spoonfuls of filling on *popiah* skin. Fold in the two sides and roll up the spring roll tightly. Seal with cornstarch water.

8. Heat oil in the same pan over medium heat and deep-fry spring rolls until golden brown and crispy.

9. Remove from heat, then drain dry and transfer spring rolls to a plate lined with absorbent paper towels.

10. Serve warm with sweet sauce.

Kueh Pie Ti

MAKES 80 PIECES

KUEH PIE TI CUPS

50 g rice flour

130 g all-purpose flour

$^1/_4$ tsp salt

$^1/_4$ tsp ground white pepper

2 eggs, beaten

$1^1/_2$ Tbsp butter, melted

300 ml water

cooking oil as needed

TURNIP FILLING
(Refer to recipe on page 96)

TOPPING (AS DESIRED)

egg omelette

shrimps or crabmeat

parsley

fried shallots

chillies, thinly sliced

ground peanuts

1. In a large bowl, mix rice flour with all-purpose flour. Add salt and pepper, then add eggs and melted butter. *(Steps 2–3 on page 99)*

2. Make a well in the centre and pour in water, a little at a time, and mix well to obtain a smooth batter. Set aside for 30 minutes before use. *(Step 4 on page 99)*

3. Heat oil in a deep wok over high heat.

4. Preheat *kueh pie ti* mould by dipping it into hot oil to get it very hot. Remove from oil and dip into batter so that the batter covers three-quarters of mould. *(Steps 5–7 on page 99)*

5. Return *kueh pie ti* mould back into the oil and deep-fry until batter sets. *(Steps 8–9 on page 99)*

6. Using a fork, gently separate *kueh pie ti* cup from the mould and fry it until light brown. Repeat until all batter is used up.

7. Remove from heat and transfer *kueh pie ti* cups to a plate lined with absorbent paper towels.

8. Drain well and cool thoroughly before storing in clean, airtight container.

9. To serve, fill *kueh pie ti* cup with turnip filling and desired toppings of omelette and shrimps or crabmeat. Complement with a small piece of parsley, fried shallots, chilli and ground peanuts.

TIP

• It is important that the moulds are hot before dipping them into the batter as the heat ensures that the batter adheres tightly to the mould. Dipping the mould into the batter immediately also helps to cook a thin layer of the *kueh pie ti* cups.

• The *kueh pie ti* cups can be stored for 1 month.

Ngoh Hiang

MAKES 6 ROLLS

dried beancurd skin as needed, cut into 6 sheets of 18 x 18-cm

1 Tbsp egg white

bread crumbs or biscuit crumbs as needed

cooking oil as needed

1 Tbsp cornflour

NGOH HIANG

150 g minced pork

150 g prawns, shelled, deveined and minced

$^1/_2$ onion, peeled and chopped

4 water chestnuts, peeled and chopped

100 g cabbage, shredded

$^1/_2$ carrot, shredded

SEASONING

1 tsp light soy sauce

3 drops dark soy sauce

1 Tbsp oyster sauce

$^1/_2$ tsp ground white pepper

$^1/_4$ tsp five-spice powder

$^1/_8$ tsp salt

$^1/_2$ tsp sugar

1. In a large bowl, combine *ngoh hiang* ingredients and mix well.

2. Add seasoning and mix well.

3. Spoon mixture onto a sheet of beancurd skin. Fold in the two sides and roll up tightly. Repeat until mixture is used up.

4. Place in steamer and steam for 10 minutes.

5. Remove from steamer and coat *ngoh hiang* with egg white and bread crumbs or biscuit crumbs.

6. Heat oil in a pan over medium heat and deep-fry *ngoh hiang* until brown.

7. Remove from heat and drain oil before transferring *ngoh hiang* to a plate lined with absorbent paper towels. Set aside to cool.

8. When cool enough to handle, divide the 6 rolls of *ngoh hiang* into serving portions and serve with chilli sauce and sweet sauce.

Nyonya Steamed Pumpkin Cake

MAKES ONE 23-CM SQUARE CAKE

oil as needed

3 Tbsp shallots, peeled and diced

2 Tbsp garlic, peeled and chopped

80 g dried shrimps

600 g pumpkin, peeled and shredded

200 g minced pork

6 Chinese mushrooms, finely diced

300 g rice flour

80 g tapioca flour

500 ml water

SEASONING

400 ml chicken or pork bone stock or 400 ml water + 1 chicken or pork stock cube

1 Tbsp sugar

1 tsp salt

1 tsp pepper

GARNISH

2 Tbsp parsley, chopped

1 Tbsp chilli, sliced

2 Tbsp fried shallots

1 tsp white sesame seeds

1. Line a 23-cm square cake tin with baking paper and brush lightly with oil. Set aside.

2. Heat oil in a pan and fry shallots, garlic and dried shrimps until fragrant.

3. Add shredded pumpkin and fry for 5 minutes before adding minced pork and Chinese mushrooms.

4. In a bowl, combine seasoning ingredients and mix well, then add to pan.

5. In a separate bowl, combine rice flour and tapioca flour with water and mix well.

6. Pour mixture into pan and continue stirring until the ingredients are pasty.

7. Transfer pumpkin mixture into prepared tin and steam over high heat for 50 minutes.

8. Remove pumpkin cake from heat and leave aside to cool on a wire rack.

9. Cut into desired number of slices and serve with chopped parsley, chilli, fried shallots and white sesame seeds.

10. Pumpkin cake can be kept refrigerated for 3 days.

TIP
- An alternative way of preparing this dish is to cut the pumpkin cake into slices when chilled and pan-fry them.

- It is important to stir continuously after the flour mixture has been added to ensure that the mixture does not burn at the bottom of the pan.

Nyonya Steamed Yam Cake

MAKES ONE 20-CM SQUARE CAKE

oil as needed

50 g Chinese mushrooms, soaked for 30 minutes in 250 g water

50 g dried shrimps, soaked for 10 minutes

300 g yam, washed and skin removed

½ cup cooking oil

100 g shallots, peeled and thinly sliced

1 tsp minced garlic

150 g minced pork or chicken

600 ml pork or chicken stock

200 g rice flour

SEASONING
1 Tbsp sugar

½ tsp five-spice powder

½ tsp ground white pepper

1 Tbsp fish sauce

1 Tbsp soy sauce

GARNISH
2 Tbsp parsley, chopped

1 Tbsp chilli, sliced

2 Tbsp fried shallots

1. Line a 23-cm square cake tin with baking paper and brush lightly with oil. Set aside.

2. Drain soaked Chinese mushrooms and cut into cubes. Reserve mushroom water for later use.

3. Drain dried shrimps and chop coarsely.

4. Cut yam into small cubes.

5. Heat oil in a wok over medium heat and fry shallots till light brown.

6. Remove from heat and transfer shallots onto a clean plate lined with absorbent paper towels. Set aside.

7. Add garlic, Chinese mushroom cubes and dried shrimps to the same wok and fry till fragrant.

8. Add yam cubes and minced pork or chicken and fry for 5 minutes. Add seasoning ingredients, mix well and remove from heat. Set aside yam mixture.

9. Bring pork or chicken stock and reserved mushroom water to a boil in the same wok.

10. Add rice flour and stir till a smooth batter is achieved.

11. Remove from heat when the batter starts to get lumpy. Pour yam mixture into the batter and mix well.

12. Transfer yam batter into prepared tin and steam over high heat for 45 minutes.

13. Remove yam cake from heat and leave aside to cool on a wire rack.

14. Cut into desired number of slices and serve with chopped parsley, chilli and fried shallots.

15. Yam cake can be kept refrigerated for 3 days.

Pulot Panggang with Shrimp Sambal

GLUTINOUS RICE WITH SHRIMP SAMBAL

MAKES 18 PIECES

18 banana leaves, cut into 20 x 20-cm square sheets

GLUTINOUS RICE

300 g glutinous rice, soaked in water for 3-4 hours and drained

100 ml coconut milk

100 ml milk

½ tsp salt

BLUE PEA FLOWER WATER

20 blue pea flowers (*bunga telang*)or a few drops of blue food colouring

3 Tbsp water

SAMBAL FILLING

½ Tbsp *belacan*

150 g dried shrimps, soaked in water for 15 minutes

4 Tbsp fresh chilli paste

20 small onions, peeled and minced

10 cloves garlic, peeled and minced

1 tsp coriander powder

½ tsp turmeric powder

1 Tbsp light soy sauce

60 ml tamarind water

½ cup cooking oil

sugar and salt to taste

1. Prepare glutinous rice. In a large bowl, mix glutinous rice, coconut milk, milk and salt. Steam mixture for 30 minutes.

2. While rice is steaming, prepare blue pea flower water. Rinse and pound flowers with a mortar and pestle. Add water and mix. Squeeze pounded flowers to extract as much juice as possible.

3. Stir rice gently with a fork and sprinkle randomly with blue pea flower water or blue food colouring. Steam for another 10 minutes.

4. Prepare sambal filling. Pound *belacan* in mortar and pestle until a fine paste is obtained. In a wok, roast *belacan* paste lightly. Remove from wok and set aside on a clean plate.

5. Heat a little oil in the same wok over medium heat and fry dried shrimps, chilli paste, small onions and minced garlic with roasted *belacan* paste, coriander powder, turmeric powder and light soy sauce. Fry till fragrant.

6. To get tamarind water, mix 1 Tbsp tamarind paste with 60 ml water.

7. Add tamarind water to the wok and season to taste with sugar and salt.

8. Reduce heat and continue frying and stirring until ingredients are dry and contain little moisture.

9. Remove sambal filling from heat and transfer to a plate. Divide sambal filling into 18 portions.

10. Heat banana leaves in oven or scald in hot water until they soften.

11. Place a tablespoonful of glutinous rice on one edge of a banana leaf, spreading it along the leaf with the back of a spoon. Put some sambal filling in the centre and cover with another tablespoonful of glutinous rice.

12. Roll and wrap banana leaf nicely in a cylindrical form and secure with bamboo toothpicks. Repeat with the rest of the glutinous rice and filling.

13. Brush packages with a little oil and grill in the oven for 8 minutes.

14. Serve hot. *Pulot panggang* can be stored for 2 days.

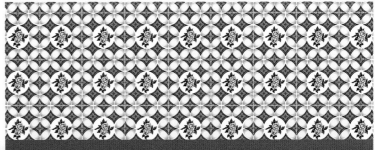

HOT AND COLD DESSERTS

Tau Suan

SPLIT MUNG BEAN SOUP

SERVES 5

250 g split mung beans

1.4 litres water

5 pandan leaves, rinsed and knotted

130 g yellow rock sugar

30 g sweet potato starch

4 fried dough fritters, cut into small pieces

1. Wash and soak split mung beans in a basin of water for at least 2 hours or overnight. Drain well.

2. In a pot, steam split mung beans for 30 minutes.

3. In a separate pot, boil 1.3 litres water, pandan leaves and rock sugar. Add split mung beans and simmer for about 30 minutes. Remove pandan leaves.

4. Mix sweet potato starch with 100 ml water and pour into the pot slowly while gently stirring the split mung beans. Boil for another 10 minutes.

5. Remove from heat and serve with fried dough fritters.

TIP

- Steaming the split mung beans before boiling will shorten the cooking time and also add more fragrance to the soup.

- It is important to stir the soup continuously after adding potato starch to ensure that the soup is not too thick and starchy.

Pulot Hitam with Sweet Potato

BLACK GLUTINOUS RICE WITH SWEET POTATO

SERVES 5

250 g black glutinous rice

1 litre water

10 pandan leaves, rinsed and knotted

180 g yellow rock sugar

$^1/_4$ tsp salt

50 ml coconut cream

1 sweet potato, steamed, peeled and cut into cubes

1. Wash and soak black glutinous rice for at least 2 hours or overnight.

2. Bring water, pandan leaves and glutinous rice to a boil in a pot. Simmer for an hour.

3. Add rock sugar and salt. Simmer for another 15 minutes until the glutinous rice grains are soft.

4. Serve with coconut cream and sweet potato cubes.

TIP

• Stir the glutinous rice regularly as the starch content of the glutinous rice can easily cause it to burn at the bottom of the pot.

• Add more water if the mixture gets too thick.

• You may substitute the coconut cream with vanilla or yam flavoured ice-cream.

Bubur Sago Terigu

WHITE WHEAT PORRIDGE WITH SAGO COCONUT CREAM

SERVES 5

300 g white wheat

3 litres water

10 pandan leaves, rinsed and knotted

300 g yellow rock sugar

$1/4$ tsp salt

2 Tbsp sago pearls, soaked for 15 minutes

150 ml coconut cream

50 ml *gula melaka* syrup

1. Soak white wheat overnight.

2. Boil water and pandan leaves in a pot. Add white wheat and simmer over low heat for an hour. Stir regularly to ensure that the mixture is smooth and not lumpy.

3. Add rock sugar and salt. Simmer for another 15 minutes until the grains are soft.

4. Add soaked sago and cook for 5 minutes until sago pearls are translucent.

5. Remove from heat.

6. Serve with coconut cream and *gula melaka* syrup.

TIP

- Stir the white wheat in the pot regularly to ensure that the mixture is smooth and not lumpy and also to prevent the mixture from burning at the bottom of the pot.

- Add more water if the mixture gets too thick.

- You may add steamed sweet potatoes or yam cubes for extra flavour and texture.

Yam Paste with Gingko Nuts and Longan

SERVES 6

600 g yam
180 g sugar
120 g peanut oil
100 g gingko nuts
1 can longans
200 ml coconut cream
maraschino cherry, for decoration

1. Peel yam and cut into chunky pieces. Steam until soft. Mash yam with a fork while it is still hot.

2. Heat wok and cook yam paste, sugar and peanut oil over medium heat until mixture is pasty and does not stick to the wok.

3. Lightly grease a clean bowl and decorate base with gingko nuts.

4. Pour yam paste into bowl and press gently to compact.

5. Overturn bowl onto a serving plate to unmould yam paste. Decorate with longans and maraschino cherry.

6. Pour coconut cream at the side of the yam paste.

7. Serve hot or cold.

TIP

- Mashing the yam while it is still hot makes it easier to remove the main vein in the root.
- Stirring the yam paste continuously will prevent it from burning at the bottom of the pan.
- Pairing the yam paste with vanilla ice cream is a delicious option.

Red Bean Kee Chang Soup

RED BEAN SOUP WITH LYE WATER RICE DUMPLINGS

SERVES 5

300 g red beans, soaked for at least an hour and drained

5 pandan leaves, rinsed and knotted

2 dried mandarin peels

1.8 litres water + more if necessary

200 g yellow rock sugar

3 *kee chang*, cut into small triangles *(Refer to recipe on page 78)*

1. Boil red beans, pandan leaves, dried mandarin peels and water in a pot for about 30 minutes.

2. Add rock sugar and simmer for another 30 minutes until red beans are broken up and soft. Add more water if the soup is too dry. Stir soup occasionally to prevent red beans from burning at the bottom of the pot.

3. Add *kee chang* into pot. Boil for another 10 minutes.

4. Remove from heat. Serve hot or cold.

TIP

- *Kee chang* can also be substituted with 3 Tbsp glutinous rice or sago.

- If desired, lotus seeds or lily bulbs can also be added at step 1 for additional taste.

Green Bean Sago Soup

SERVES 5

300 g green beans, soaked for 30 minutes and drained

5 pandan leaves, rinsed and knotted

1.8 litres water

150 g yellow rock sugar

100 g sago pearls

60 ml coconut milk (optional)

1. Bring green beans, pandan leaves and water to a boil in a pot, and boil for 30 minutes.

2. Add rock sugar and simmer until green beans are broken up and soft. Stir occasionally to prevent soup from burning at the bottom of the pot.

3. In a small bowl, soak sago for 15 minutes and drain well. Add sago into the pot containing green beans.

4. Boil for 5 minutes until sago pearls are translucent and cooked.

5. Remove from heat. Serve hot or cold with coconut milk (optional).

TIP

- If preferred, sago can also be substituted with 2 Tbsp glutinous rice. Introduce glutinous rice in the first step, when bringing green beans, pandan leaves and water to the boil.

- Green bean soup has the additional health benefit of dispelling toxins and reducing heat in the body.

White Fungus and Longan Soup

80 g white fungus

10 sterculia seeds
(*pang da hai*)

100 g yellow rock sugar

1.8 litres water

100 g lotus seeds

100 g gingko nuts

150 g dried longans

1. Soak white fungus in water until it expands. Drain well and trim away the hard stems.

2. Soak sterculia seeds for 30 minutes until they expand. Remove all the skin of the seeds.

3. Bring rock sugar and water to a boil in a pot, and boil until sugar is completely dissolved.

4. Add white fungus, lotus seeds and gingko nuts and boil for about 30 minutes. Add dried longans and sterculia seeds and boil for another 10 minutes.

5. Remove from heat. Serve hot or cold.

TIP
- Sterculia seeds can be bought at traditional Chinese medical halls.

Red Rubies with Jackfruit

SERVES 5

20 water chestnuts, washed, peeled and cut into small cubes

a few drops of red colouring or rose syrup

80 g tapioca flour

6 pandan leaves, rinsed and knotted

100 ml coconut milk

100 ml milk

a pinch of salt

50 g sago pearls, soaked

5 pieces jackfruit, cut into cubes

SUGAR SYRUP
4 Tbsp sugar
100 ml water

1. Put water chestnuts into a plastic bag. Add a few drops of red colouring or rose syrup into bag.

2. Shake and mix water chestnuts well until they are evenly coated with the red colouring.

3. Add tapioca flour into bag. Shake and toss plastic bag well until water chestnuts are evenly coated with the tapioca flour.

4. Boil pandan leaves in a pot of water. Gently lower water chestnuts into pot and boil until they rise to the surface. Pour away the water from pot.

5. Prepare a big bowl of ice water. Scoop water chestnuts out and place into ice water to stop the cooking process. Keep chestnuts in ice water until required.

6. Boil coconut milk and milk with a pinch of salt in the same pot for 10 minutes. Add soaked sago and sugar. Cook until sago pearls are translucent.

7. Fill bowls with coconut milk and milk mixture. Top with water chestnuts and jackfruit cubes.

8. Prepare sugar syrup. Add sugar to water and mix well.

9. Add sugar syrup to serving bowls, then adjust according to your desired sweetness.

TIP
- If you prefer the rubies to have a thicker coating, toss the water chestnuts in tapioca flour twice: once before the rubies are wet and once after the rubies are wet.

- Corn and *chendol* jelly strips can be added to the recipe for a greater variety of colours.

Bubor Cha Cha

SWEET POTATO, YAM AND TAPIOCA CUBES IN COCONUT SAGO CREAM

SERVES 6

130 g tapioca flour

a pinch of salt

40 ml boiling water

a few drops each of purple, pink, yellow and green food colouring

500 ml coconut milk

500 ml milk

120 g yellow rock sugar

$1/4$ tsp salt

4 Tbsp sago pearls, soaked

300 g sweet potatoes, skinned, steamed and cut into cubes

300 g yam, skinned, steamed and cut into cubes

1. Prepare tapioca cubes. Combine tapioca flour and salt in a mixing bowl. Add boiling water and stir to mix well. Set aside for 10 minutes.

2. When mixture is cool enough to handle, knead to form a soft dough. Continue kneading until dough is pliable and springy.

3. Divide dough into 5 portions and add enough colouring to each portion, leaving 1 portion uncoloured. Knead each portion well to blend the colouring and dough together. Roll each portion into long strips and cut into 1-cm cubes.

4. Bring a big pot of water to the boil. Gently add tapioca cubes and boil until they are translucent and rise to the surface.

5. Prepare a big bowl of ice water. Scoop tapioca cubes out and place into ice water to stop the cooking process. Keep tapioca cubes in ice water until required.

6. In a separate bowl, combine coconut milk, milk, rock sugar and salt and boil for 10 minutes, stirring until sugar dissolves. Add soaked sago and cook until sago pearls are translucent.

7. Remove from heat. Add sweet potatoes, yam and tapioca cubes and stir to mix well.

8. Serve hot or cold.

TIP
- The coloured tapioca cubes can be replaced with big sago pearls.
- Store-bought tapioca cubes can also be used. Prepare according to instructions.

Gula Melaka Sago Dessert

PALM SUGAR SAGO DESSERT

SERVES 5

200 g sago, washed and soaked for 15 minutes

125 ml coconut milk + more to serve

125 ml milk

5 pandan leaves, rinsed and knotted

1/4 tsp salt

coconut milk to serve

GULA MELAKA SYRUP

200 g palm sugar (*gula melaka*)

50 ml water

1. Cook soaked sago in a big pot of water for 10 minutes until translucent.

2. Remove from heat and strain to drain away excess starch water.

3. Brush a 4-cm mini tart tray with oil and pour sago into the moulds. Set aside to cool and refrigerate.

4. Boil coconut milk, milk, pandan leaves and salt in a pot. Cool and set aside.

5. In another pot, cook palm sugar and water over low heat until the sugar dissolves.

6. Serve sago pudding with *gula melaka* syrup and coconut milk.

TIP

• Do not stir the sago while soaking as this will dissolve the sago pearls.

• When cooking, stir the sago continuously to ensure that the mixture is smooth and not lumpy.

Nyonya Crisp Agar-agar

SERVES 8

80 g agar-agar strips, soaked in water for 15 minutes

5 pandan leaves, rinsed and knotted

800 g yellow rock sugar

3 litres water

a few drops each of red and green food colouring

1. Bring agar-agar strips and pandan leaves to a boil in a pot, and boil for 30 minutes over low heat until agar-agar dissolves.

2. Add rock sugar and continue to simmer for another 30 minutes, stirring until sugar dissolves. Remove pandan leaves.

3. Remove from heat and divide mixture into 2 portions. Stir in a different food colouring in each portion.

4. Pour into trays or moulds. Chill mixture in refrigerator until agar-agar sets.

5. Cut agar-agar into desired number of slices using a serrated knife.

6. Dry in the sun for 2 days or until agar-agar is crisp and very crunchy. Store in clean, dry airtight jars. Agar-agar can be refrigerated for 6 months.

TIP

- Remove the foam that rises to the surface of the agar-agar mixture during simmering to prevent the foam from solidifying on the agar-agar surface and also to ensure that the surface remains smooth.

- If preferred, half of the sugar can be replaced with *gula melaka* for additional taste.

Banana and Corn Nagasari

BANANA AND CORN HOON KUEH

MAKES 25 PIECES

25 banana leaves, cut into 25 cm x 20-cm rectangular sheets

60 g mung bean flour

130 g yellow rock sugar

200 g canned creamed corn

2.1 litres coconut milk

2.1 litres milk

$^1/_4$ tsp salt

5 pandan leaves, rinsed and knotted

5 bananas, peeled and sliced into small pieces

1. Heat banana leaves in oven or scald in hot water to soften them.

2. Drain well. When cool enough to handle, grease banana leaves. Set aside.

3. In a pot, combine mung bean flour, rock sugar, creamed corn, coconut milk, milk, salt and pandan leaves and bring to a boil.

4. Cook over low heat for 30 minutes, stirring constantly to ensure that the mixture is smooth and not lumpy. Remove pandan leaves.

5. Remove from heat.

6. Ladle 2 tablespoons of creamed corn mixture onto the banana leaf and place a slice of banana on top.

7. Fold the 2 long edges over each other, then tuck the other two edges underneath to form a rectangular pack. Repeat until mixture is used up.

8. Chill in refrigerator and serve cold.

TIP
- Cook the mixture longer for a crunchy texture. Stir the mixture regularly to prevent the mixture from burning at the bottom.
- Wrap the mixture fast as it will set in 5 minutes.

Equipment

Chiffon cake tin

Kitchen scraper

Kueh pie ti mould

Pineapple tart mould

Tart moulds

Pulot tai tai moulds

Pastry pincers

Serrated knife for agar-agar

Star mould

Mini tart moulds

Palette knife

Daisy butter cookie mould

Oven Mode

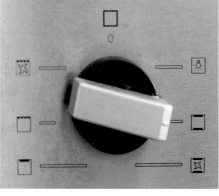

- Top and Bottom (double lines only) – For single-tier baking (cakes, especially dry cakes like sponge and chiffon cakes.)

- Top and Bottom (double lines with fan) – For multi-tier or tray baking (cakes, especially rich cakes like muffins, puff pastries and cookies.)

- Grill (with fan) – For even roasting and grilling (whole bird or meat with a lot of juices or interval sauce brushing.)

- Grill (no fan) – For small items e.g. satays and kebabs and special cakes like *kueh lapis*

- Grill (centre only) – For small quantity of food.

Bundt cake pan

Whisk

Brush

Sago dessert mould

Rolling pin

Grater

Spatula

Kueh bangkit moulds

Parchment bags

Ang ku kueh mould

Kueh bolu mould

Glossary of Ingredients

Black glutinous rice

Belacan

Dried wintermelon

Dried shrimps

Galangal

Bamboo leaves

Glutinous rice

Banana leaves

Bamboo strings

Hoisin sauce

Kaffir lime leaves

Gingko nuts

Gula melaka syrup and
gula melaka

Blue pea flowers

Candlenuts

Coconut cream

Hua tiao wine/Chinese wine

Dried beancurd skin

141

Sterculia seeds

Sago pearls

Mung bean flour

Sago flour

Maltose

Alkaline water and orange lye

Lemongrass

Pandan leaves

Tamarind pulp

Turmeric

Vanilla essence and powder

Wheat starch flour

Semolina flour

Turmeric leaf

Weights and Measures

Quantities for this book are given in Metric, Imperial and American (spoon) measures. Standard spoon and cup measurements used are: 1 tsp = 5 ml, 1 Tbsp = 15 ml, 1 cup = 250 ml. All measures are level unless otherwise stated.

LIQUID AND VOLUME MEASURES

Metric	Imperial	American
5 ml	$1/6$ fl oz	1 teaspoon
10 ml	$1/3$ fl oz	1 dessertspoon
15 ml	$1/2$ fl oz	1 tablespoon
60 ml	2 fl oz	$1/4$ cup (4 tablespoons)
85 ml	$2^1/2$ fl oz	$1/3$ cup
90 ml	3 fl oz	$3/8$ cup (6 tablespoons)
125 ml	4 fl oz	$1/2$ cup
180 ml	6 fl oz	$3/4$ cup
250 ml	8 fl oz	1 cup
300 ml	10 fl oz ($1/2$ pint)	$1^1/4$ cups
375 ml	12 fl oz	$1^1/2$ cups
435 ml	14 fl oz	$1^3/4$ cups
500 ml	16 fl oz	2 cups
625 ml	20 fl oz (1 pint)	$2^1/2$ cups
750 ml	24 fl oz ($1^1/5$ pints)	3 cups
1 litre	32 fl oz ($1^3/5$ pints)	4 cups
1.25 litres	40 fl oz (2 pints)	5 cups
1.5 litres	48 fl oz ($2^2/5$ pints)	6 cups
2.5 litres	80 fl oz (4 pints)	10 cups

DRY MEASURES

Metric	Imperial
30 grams	1 ounce
45 grams	$1^1/2$ ounces
55 grams	2 ounces
70 grams	$2^1/2$ ounces
85 grams	3 ounces
100 grams	$3^1/2$ ounces
110 grams	4 ounces
125 grams	$4^1/2$ ounces
140 grams	5 ounces
280 grams	10 ounces
450 grams	16 ounces (1 pound)
500 grams	1 pound, $1^1/2$ ounces
700 grams	$1^1/2$ pounds
800 grams	$1^1/2$ pounds
1 kilogram	2 pounds, 3 ounces
1.5 kilograms	3 pounds, $4^1/2$ ounces
2 kilograms	4 pounds, 6 ounces

OVEN TEMPERATURE

	°C	°F	Gas Regulo
Very slow	120	250	1
Slow	150	300	2
Moderately slow	160	325	3
Moderate	180	350	4
Moderately hot	190/200	370/400	5/6
Hot	210/220	410/440	6/7
Very hot	230	450	8
Super hot	250/290	475/550	9/10

LENGTH

Metric	Imperial
0.5 cm	$1/4$ inch
1 cm	$1/2$ inch
1.5 cm	$3/4$ inch
2.5 cm	1 inch